AF759000

Effective Bank Regulation and Supervision: Lessons from the Financial Crisis

By Steven I. Davis

Searching finance

First published 2010 by Searching Finance Ltd.,
8 Whitehall Road, London W7 2JE, UK

ISBN 978-1-907720-00-0

Typeset by j-views, Kamakura, Japan

Cover photo by Hugh Ashton

Effective Bank Regulation and Supervision: Lessons from the Financial Crisis

By Steven I. Davis

Searching finance

About the author

Steven I. Davis has spent his career in the banking and financial services sector as a senior executive, strategy consultant, author, analyst and teacher. He is a graduate (magna cum laude) of Amherst College and of the Harvard Business School.

His 20-year career in international banking commenced at JPMorgan, where he managed a Paris-based research and M & A unit. For Bankers Trust Company, he ran a venture capital subsidiary in New York and later the bank's European businesses from a London headquarters. Subsequently he set up and managed for six years the London-based merchant banking subsidiary of First International Bancshares of Dallas, Texas.

Since establishing Davis International Banking Consultants (DIBC) in 1980, he has managed several hundred strategy assignments for commercial and investment banks, global fund managers, insurers and other financial institutions. In 1993, he headed a DIBC team which advised the Norwegian Ministry of Finance on the restructuring of the country's banking sector during the Nordic banking crisis. In addition, he and his colleagues have prepared over 60 research reports on the financial sector for publication by investment banks and other clients.

Mr. Davis is also the author of 14 books and reports published on best practice in the financial services sector.

About Searching Finance Ltd

Searching Finance Ltd is a dynamic new voice in knowledge provision for the financial services and related professional sectors. Our mission is to provide expert, highly relevant and actionable information and analysis, written by professionals, for professionals. For more information, please visit www.searchingfinance.co.uk

Contents

Chapter 6: Politics and bank regulation

Chapter 7: Regulatory authority case studies

Chapter 9: Conclusions

Appendix: Extracts from Pillar 2 of the Basel II Accord

Bibliography

Tables and Figures

Preface

MY STARTING POINT for this research was with a telephone interview in early 2009 with Matias Inciarte, a Vice-Chairman of Banco Santander. My objective was to gather insights for another research project on the outlook for bank strategies after the financial crisis. His response to a question on the issue of regulation was "It's all about supervision, not regulation" and proceeded to praise the Bank of Spain's policy of embedding – i.e. permanently installing – its supervisors in banks like his. This triggered the memory of a comment from a senior US bank regulator about hundreds of similar supervisors embedded in major US banks being unable to mitigate the disasters which took place in such institutions.

This reinforced my view of the importance of the role of regulation or supervision in the future stability of the global banking system. Maybe the regulators had forgotten about actually enforcing their rules by effective supervision? And what about the virtues of principles-based, as opposed to rules-based regulation? Somewhere among the hundreds of bank regulators around the world should be some clues as to what works and what doesn't as the 'new normal' in bank regulation is introduced. In brief, with hundreds of bank regulatory agencies to choose from, I calculated that there must be lessons to be drawn for future best practice.

Post the financial crisis, there has been a tsunami of interest in bank regulation, which culminated at the end of 2009 in a swath of new edicts from global (Basel), regional (EU) and national regulators designed to prevent – or at least mitigate – the next global financial crisis. My personal experience has focused extensively on best practice in banking, and I felt that there could be valuable insight to be gained from taking a similar analytical approach to what represents best practice – i.e. effective and successful – banking regulation or supervision globally. I therefore undertook a series of in-depth interviews with experienced, knowledgeable executives with different perspectives on the issues – senior bankers, regulators and supervisors, academics, management consultants, rating agencies and securities analysts.

My objective was to gather as much evidence as possible of best regulatory practice under fire during the recent financial crisis to provide some thoughtful insights and positive lessons for regulators and those responsible for the regulatory function. My goal was not to opine on what the ideal form of regulation itself should be; there is already much opinion and comment from academics, journalists, present and former regulators, consultants and others. This project's aim was different: **not** to present one opinion on the *correct* approach to bank regulation, but to offer a *synthesis* of the experience of expert views on best regulatory practice revealed during the recent crisis.

My first step was to validate my approach with a number of industry participants and commentators familiar with the issues and, perhaps more important, prepared to provide an honest appraisal of my proposal. These included Ted Ladd, a senior investment manager with close contact to the US regulatory community; Gerard Legrain, a fellow former London banker with a passion for banking research; two UK academics, David Llewellyn and Phil Molyneux; and John Grammer, a fellow banking consultant. I am deeply grateful to them for their time, wisdom and introductions.

This book could not have been written without the support and insights of my colleague of many years, Brenda Jenner, and it is a special pleasure once again to have the support of Ann Tierney at Searching Finance as publisher.

Finally, I owe a deep debt of gratitude to the 31 individuals who were kind enough to take time away from their day jobs to grant me an off-the-record interview. Most are professionals deeply involved in the regulatory debate, and even speaking off the record, given the sensitivity of the issues involved, was not an easy choice.

Chapter 1: Introduction and overview

THE RECENT FINANCIAL CRISIS has unleashed a flood of views on what happened, why it happened, and what new regulatory measures and structures might prevent or mitigate such crises in the future.

Key questions

HERE WE TAKE A DIFFERENT APPROACH. Based on in-depth, off-the-record interviews with 31 senior, experienced bankers, regulators, consultants and others deeply involved in the regulatory process, we seek to answer two key questions:

1. Which bank regulators around the world have demonstrated relatively superior results in terms of regulatory outcomes; and
2. What lessons for the future can be drawn from their experience?

After summarising the unique dimensions of the crisis and the proposed re-regulatory measures now in train, we examine three key differentiators of bank regulation agencies:

- Regulatory structure;
- Professional skills; and
- The political environment in which they function.

We then profiled nine case studies of national regulation to examine the drivers of such regulatory success or failure. And finally we synthesised the experts' and our own conclusions on the likely future success of bank regulation and the key factors which are likely to determine such outcomes.

Regulatory structure

OUR ANALYSIS OF THE STRUCTURE of bank regulation confirms that there is no single best deployment in a given country of the central bank, the finance ministry, a dedicated bank supervisory authority, or other government agencies. Each structure has failed or succeeded in different ways in relative terms during the recent crisis. Yet experience has shown that the use of multiple agencies, such as a tripartite structure, for example in Norway and the UK, requires intense collaboration and information-sharing among the agencies to succeed. Gaps and overlaps are responsible for many of the recent regulatory failures.

Professional skills

AS FOR PROFESSIONAL SKILLS, the central bank and the finance ministry usually have the advantage of a sound macro-economic reputation and the ability to attract superior brainpower in the country, but they often lack the practical understanding of banking needed to identify and address key risk issues. On the other hand, specialist prudential agencies have the necessary contact with the banks, but often give priority to administrative oversight, consumer protection, and other tasks rather than the detection and addressing of systemic and individual risk issues.

Political environment

FINALLY, THE ISSUE OF POLITICAL PRESSURE and interference with the regulatory process is a significant one in a number of markets where voters can influence the legislative process so as to defend the perceived interests of a portion of the banking system. Many observers view 'politics' as one of the most serious unresolved issues in effective bank regulation.

The case studies profiled included those of dedicated bank supervisory entities in Canada, France, Italy, Australia, and Norway, which have emerged from the crisis with a successful track record in identifying systemic issues and taking proactive intervention measures to address these issues. The Bank of Spain is examined as a case study of success in proactive intervention with regard to the adequacy of loss reserves and accounting for off-balance sheet units. Case studies of bank regulation in the US, Germany and the UK demonstrate the issues of regulatory gaps, dilution of focus on risk assessment, and political intervention in the regulatory process.

As for the outlook for bank regulation, our sources generally agreed that future crises are inevitable. The unpredictability of the source of future systemic problems, the frequent influence of politics in the process, and the track record of actually implementing the long-established supervisory responsibility incorporated in Pillar 2 of the current Basel framework all point to the conclusion that bank regulation can only be expected to mitigate, not prevent, future banking problems.

Steps for improving regulatory effectiveness

BUT THE RECENT CRISIS has pointed up a number of steps which can improve regulatory effectiveness in the future. Improved collaboration among multiple regulatory agencies is one. Another is the emphasis on systemic and individual bank risk assessment as the central mission of such regulation, rather than consumer protection or administrative tasks.

Most of our sources concur in the primacy of simple 'old-fashioned' measures such as focus on a few key metrics like capital adequacy and liquidity, as well as the importance of inspection, close contact between bank CEOs and their regulatory counterparts, and, most difficult of all, proactive intervention by the regulator if needed. On the other hand, there is less confidence in the structural measures recently proposed to limit the size and profile of banks. as well as the limitation of bonuses.

In brief, the issues of regulatory structure and adequacy of professional skills can be addressed with relative ease by a determined agency, while that of political interference in a democratic environment can perhaps only be dealt with by improving the public's confidence in the regulatory mechanism as a parallel with the trust in the macro-economic management in many countries over the past few decades.

Research objective and methodology

THE OBJECTIVE OF THIS RESEARCH is to spotlight best practice in banking regulation in the context of the 2007–09 financial crisis, based on the on-the-ground experience of senior and experienced regulators, bankers, academics, management consultants, bank analysts and rating agencies. To the extent possible with such a sensitive topic, interview material is attributed to the source involved, but understandably much of it is provided off the record and anonymously. Every effort was made to obtain an interview sample with a rough balance in geographic and functional terms, as well as type of institution involved. Of necessity, given the profile of the crisis, there is heavy reliance on sources from North America and Europe.

Several questions formed the core of our interview approach:

- Can you suggest examples of successful approaches and initiatives of individual national regulators which might be relevant in a wider context?
- What are the critical dimensions of a successful national bank regulator, such as structure, quality of professional staff, and the ability to take a stand independent of public opinion? What can we learn from the mistakes made?
- How successful do you believe the suggested approach of macro-prudential regulation will be in practice in terms of preventing or mitigating future major financial crises?

- Can one identify general principles of success which should inform regulatory agencies? How have such critical issues of regulatory structure, adequacy of professional skills, and preserving independence of action been successfully addressed?

The balance of the book consists of the following chapters.

For those interested in the evolution and significance of the recent crisis, Chapter 2 provides a brief summary of its highlights. Our focus is on those significant developments which were not anticipated and are therefore of particular interest to regulators aiming to improve their performance in the future. We have relied in particular on a summary of the key failures of bank regulation and supervision provided by the highly regarded analysts at the Credit Sights agency.

Chapter 3 summarises the suggested best practice in bank regulation as articulated recently at three levels: global (by the Basel Committee); regional (by the EU's Committee on Banking Supervision); and national (as outlined by Ben Bernanke of the US Federal Reserve Board). This approach is commonly termed 'macro-prudential' (essentially, extending the traditional focus on an individual bank to broader, or systemic, developments across the banking sector) as a parallel with the macroeconomic stance of central bankers which focuses on systemic issues. It is contrasted with Pillar 2 of the existing Basel II structure which describes the role of supervisory agencies in dealing with systemic issues.

Chapter 4 is the first of three designed to analyse individual issues using the input from our interview series and other material. The chapter addresses the basic issue of institutional structure by evaluating the choice of single vs. multiple agencies, problems of communication among agencies, and the relative merits of the role of the central bank or other agency as a bank regulator. The chapter also discusses the relative role of regulation (making the rules) as opposed to supervision (enforcing the rules) as a possible issue in effectiveness.

Chapter 5 deals with the issue of professional skills. We record the views of our interview sample on the subjects of the relative skills needed for success in bank regulation and supervision, the mandate given to regulators and supervisors, the availability of such skills, and the best means of ensuring access to the limited pool of relevant talent.

Our analysis of critical success factors in bank regulation concludes in Chapter 6 with a discussion of the issue of dealing with political opposition to regulatory action. Each national market differs from its peers in a number of dimensions, and so-called 'politics' has been a major national differentiator. We discuss the drivers of success – and failure – in this critical dimension.

Chapter 7 profiles as case studies a number of national markets or agencies and their relative success in dealing with the regulatory challenge. Several of these markets and agencies have been selected as relative success stories by our interviewees; others have emerged from our own analysis as interesting role models, and a few others have been selected as agencies or national structures which have been subjected to particular criticism during the crisis. The selection is not designed to be a league table of regulatory success or failure. Our intent is rather to highlight the critical success factors described in the preceding three chapters.

The views of our interviewees on the likely course of bank regulation in the future are detailed in Chapter 8. A particular focus is placed on the possible success of macro-prudential regulation in addressing systemic issues in the future.

Chapter 9 concludes with our own views on the outlook for successful bank regulation.

Research participants

Institutions

APRA (Australian Prudential Regulatory Authority)
Banca de España
Banca d'Italia
BNY Mellon
BaFin (Federal Financial Supervisory Authority)
Bankinter
Banque de France/Commission Bancaire
Boston Consulting Group
CBFA (Commission Bancaire, Financière et des Assurances)
Citibank
Deutsche Bank
Fitch Ratings
Financial Services Authority (UK)
Financial Supervisory Authority of Norway
HSBC
Lloyds Banking Group
Oliver Wyman
McKinsey & Co
OSFI (Office of the Superintendent of Financial Institutions)
Office of the Comptroller of the Currency
Promontory Financial Group
Sandler O'Neill
State Street Bank
Swedbank

Individuals

Claudio Borio
Clive Briault
Professor James Barth

Larry Fish
Edward Ladd
Professor David Llewellyn

Chapter 2: Anatomy of the banking crisis

"Collective and pervasive blindness...knowledge obstacles... phenomena that were either ignored or downplayed in importance" (Mario Draghi, Chairman of Financial Stability Board and Governor of the Bank of Italy, in a presentation in November 2009)

"The root cause of the cycle is collective human behaviour – unbridled optimism on the upside and fear – bordering on panic on the downside ... it is virtually impossible to anticipate when optimism gives rise to fear or fear gives rise to optimism" (Letter to Henry Paulson, Secretary of the Treasury, from the Counterparty Risk Management Group, August 2008)

Overview

MARIO DRAGHI'S SPEECH in November 2009 neatly summarises what happened in the global financial crisis which burst on the scene in mid-2007. But it must be taken in its historical context going back to the early days of banking and capital markets. Required reading for any student of banking crises is Charles Kindleberger's seminal work, 'Manias, Panics and Crashes', which tracks the innumerable banking disasters – invariably following an asset price bubble – going back to the 17th century and tulip mania. Over the years a succession of such panics led to the emergence of a national lender of last resort, often a central bank such as the Bank of England or Banque de France, which might or might not actually stem the crisis by providing the necessary funds.

The US finally followed the European lead, with the formation, after extended political debate, of the Federal Reserve System in 1913 to replace leading bankers like JPMorgan which had played that role in the 1907 Bankers' Panic – a financial crisis that occurred when the New York Stock Exchange fell close to 50% from its peak the previous year resulting in numerous runs on banks and trust companies and many state and local banks and businesses becoming bankrupt. Yet reading JM Keynes' masterful study of the Great Depression of the 1930s confirmed that the mere presence of a central bank was not sufficient to restore stability and growth.

Another piece of required reading is Robert Shiller's seminal study on financial cycles, 'Irrational Exuberance', which slices and dices stock market cycles over an extended period of time to disprove the notion that such cycles can be predicted. His conclusion: markets rise and fall, but the timing and extent of these movements is beyond the wit of man.

And the final piece of fascinating reading is the outcome of the 2007–8 global banking crisis, 'Too Big to Fail', by Andrew Ross Sorkin, a remarkable blow-by-blow narrative of the near-collapse of the US financial system in the fall of 2008.

Key developments in the financial crisis

WHILE COUNTLESS FORESTS have been felled to describe and analyse this most recent crisis, it may be useful to summarise very briefly its key elements as a prelude to the chapters which follow, based on the excellent summary of unexpected financial disasters of the past decade prepared by the analysts at the US research firm Credit Sights. Those who are only too familiar with the crisis, however, are encouraged to skip to Chapter 3.

Four particular – and unexpected – developments played a central role in the crisis.

- Macro-economic dislocation;
- The explosion of sub-prime lending in the US;
- Lack of transparency and management and regulatory controls; and
- Market panics and the drying-up of liquidity.

Macro-economic dislocation

THE CHARTS FROM CONSULTANTS McKinsey & Co below profile the macro-economic dislocation by the end of 2006 which set the stage for the crisis. Vast balance of payments differentials between the US and the emerging markets, significant new financial players and products, as well as the 'shadow', or non-bank banking system, were apparent (see further Chapter 3). International bodies such as the International Monetary Fund (IMF) documented these danger signals. The stage was set, however, for a perceived global 'wall of money' seeking employment and superior returns.

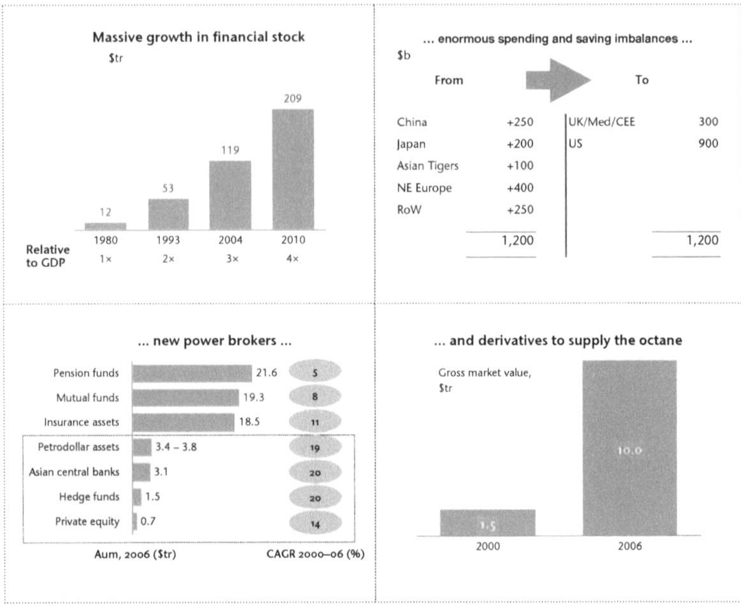

Figure 2.1: *Global financial system built to bubble*

Source: McKinsey & Co
International Bank Planners Forum Presentation, November 2007

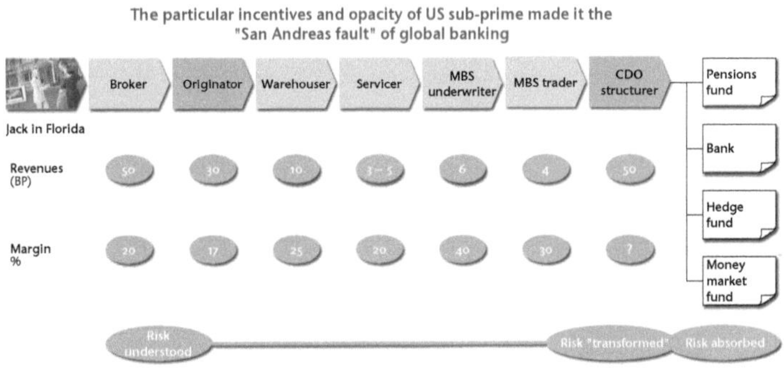

Figure 2.2: *US sub-prime – the 'San Andreas fault' of global banking*

Source: McKinsey & Co
International Bank Planners Forum Presentation, November 2007

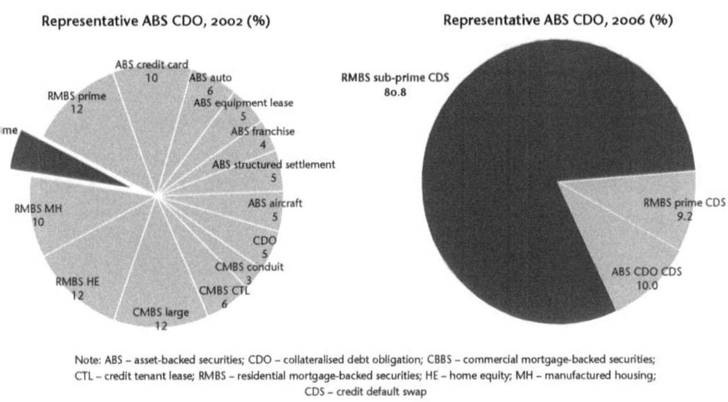

Figure 2.3: *CDOs become highly concentrated ....*

Source: McKinsey & Co
International Bank Planners Forum Presentation, November 2007

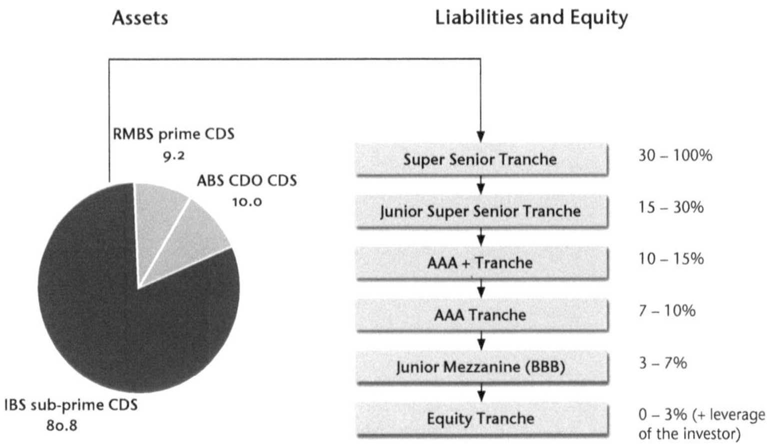

Figure 2.4: ... *and highly leveraged*

Source: McKinsey & Co
International Bank Planners Forum Presentation, November 2007

The explosion of sub-prime lending in the US

BOOMING HOUSE PRICES in the US and a mortgage sector without the constraints present in other markets such as maximum LTV (loan to value) ratios and personal guarantees of mortgage indebtedness, attracted a host of non-bank intermediaries, who created, packaged, leveraged and sold such mortgages as CDOs (collateralised debt obligations) to end-buyers around the world. Using valuation models based on optimistic price scenarios, these intermediaries persuaded the leading rating agencies to award AAA ratings to such products, with the result that over half of the US mortgages created by 2007 were held by investors and institutions outside the US. As losses were realised on the sub-prime loans constituting the equity portion of such CDOs, their ratings and valuations collapsed.

To quote Credit Sights:

"The 'AAA turnstile' took some of the higher risk vehicles being designed and manufactured by the Street and handed them to a next generation turbocharger to drive more volume through an increasingly leveraged system...the quirks of the bank regulations on external ratings fed the beast ... the thought seemed to be 'give me a AAA rating that trades as a BBB spread and I will buy it all day!' For example, when a German bank gets crushed by underlying assets such as Florida and California residential housing, we are seeing the downside of financial globalisation."

Lack of transparency and management and regulatory controls

INVESTMENT BANKING IS NOT A TRANSPARENT BUSINESS, and intermediaries such as Lehman Brothers and Bear Stearns acquired massive amounts of such sub-prime based products and financed them on the short-term repo market in New York. As Credit Sights points out:

"Lehman Brothers could be the ultimate symbol ... of unbridled growth in counterparty risk and lax risk controls, poor disclosure in the brokerage industry, and proof that the need to 'print tickets' will always take precedence over ... risk management. It was the ultimate gut check on how bad disclosure really was in the banking and brokerage sector."

Market panics and the drying-up of liquidity

TWO FAILURES – Northern Rock in the UK and Lehman Brothers in the US – were triggered by market panic and a disappearance of liquidity. A mid-sized UK retail bank, the collapse of Northern Rock in mid-2007 was the first indication that markets – specifically the securitised bond market which funded Northern Rock – could melt away under stress. The bankruptcy of Lehman Brothers in 2008, following exhaustive but unsuccessful efforts by the US authorities to find a buyer, became the first major US bank to fail and triggered a panic collapse of US bank stocks. A credit crisis had thus morphed into a liquidity collapse. The resulting 'death spiral' in both the US and UK – with equity values collapsing daily – resulted in the massive injection – estimated at US$1trn – of public funds globally to refloat the banks under attack.

Chapter 3: The emerging new model of financial regulation

"No firm, by virtue of its size and complexity, should be permitted to hold the financial system, the economy, or the American taxpayer hostage" (Statement by Ben Bernanke, Chairman of the Federal Reserve, December 2009)

THE EPICENTRE OF the banking crisis was the US, and the above quotation from a speech by the Chairman of the US Fed epitomises the urgency of the US programme to address the issues raised by the crisis.

The final weeks of 2009 saw a remarkable flood of new regulatory initiatives, structures and work programmes across the global banking sector. We summarise first the overall structures, followed by the key features of the new drivers of bank regulation. We conclude with a more detailed look at the implantation process which has begun in recent months.

New regulatory structures across the three geographic levels of bank supervision

WHILE NATIONAL AGENCIES remain central to the bank regulatory process, the role of global and, to a lesser extent, regional structures has become increasingly important. Conceptually, global bodies such as the Basel Committee will agree policy with decisions to be made by local supervisors, who will ensure implementation of the rules and scrutinise local banking institutions. In the EU, a series of committees seeks to ensure a consistent approach. The three key dimensions of the structure are:

- **Global,** in the form of the existing Basel Committee on Banking Supervision and the new Financial Stability Board (FSB), which was established to address vulnerabilities and to develop and implement strong regulatory, supervisory and other policies in the interest of financial stability. The FSB was created following the 2009 G20 meeting.
- **Regional,** in the European Union's new Supervisory Board that brings together senior regulators from the 27

member countries. There are some 49 national authorities in the EU which have supervisory responsibility for banking, securities or insurance firms, and the new Committee of European Banking Supervisors will consist of lead national authorities in each of the 27 EU countries.

- **National** initiatives in major markets like the US and UK. There has been active discussion of possible restructuring of regulation in several national markets but no major changes to date. As discussed in Chapter 4 on regulatory structure, gaps and overlaps have been revealed in these structures.

New initiatives in bank regulation

MUCH MORE SIGNIFICANT are the new initiatives triggered by the financial crisis. The major themes on the agenda in early 2010 are summarised below.

- **Extending the perimeter of bank regulation** to entities which function to extend credit or otherwise provide banking services. This so-called 'shadow' banking system can include investment banks and brokers, SIVs (structured investment vehicles), mortgage brokers, finance companies, insurers, hedge funds and private equity firms. Investment banks and brokers are the particular focus of interest in this collection of non-bank financial institutions.
- **Increasing the amount and quality of capital.** Widespread agreement has already been reached on the need to increase the proportion of Tier 1 capital as well as its quality, by eliminating quasi-equity funds from the equation to create so-called core Tier 1 capital.
- **Establishing a maximum leverage ratio.** In many national markets, the ratio of total assets to capital soared during the pre-2007 boom period as banks ballooned

their earning assets without necessarily violating their Tier 1 guidelines, which are based on risk-weighted assets. Such a leverage cap would appear to be a likely outcome of the current debate.

- **Setting up a so-called 'resolution authority'** for institutions that are perceived to be 'too big to fail' and thus likely to be bailed out by the national authorities. The current debate centres on so-called 'living wills' which set out in advance the methodology by which a troubled bank can be broken up without the chaos which followed the collapse of Lehman Brothers in 2008.
- **Counter-cyclical provisions and similar actions** to offset the pro-cyclical nature of banking growth. This has focused on across-the-cycle loan loss provisioning as opposed to the current policy – mandated by the accounting profession – of establishing a provision only when the loan is deemed to be non-performing.
- **Limiting bank bonuses.** The wave of public anger over bank bailouts from taxpayer funds has focused attention on the timing, amount and nature (cash or stock) of bank compensation.

The overall theme of macro-prudential supervision

MANY OF THESE TOPICS are encompassed by the concept of macro-prudential supervision. Envisaged as a parallel to the well-established central banking practice of macro-economic policy – essentially managing interest rates and the money supply – it has arisen because of the failure of many national authorities to identify and act upon macro or systemic issues such as liquidity, the need to dampen loan demand, gaps in regulatory coverage, individual 'toxic' products like sub-prime which represent a risk to clients and the system, and others which extend beyond the regulation of individual banking institutions.

	Macro-prudential	Micro-prudential
Proximate objective	Limit financial system-wide distress	Limit distress of individual institutions
Ultimate objective	Avoid output (GDP) costs	Consumer (investor/ depositor protection
Characterisation of risk	Seen as independent on collective behaviour ('endogenous')	Seen as independent of individual agents' behaviour ('exogenous')
Correlations and common exposures across institutions	Important	Irrelevant
Calibration of prudential controls	In terms of system-wide risk; top-down	In terms of risks of individual institutions; bottom-up

Table 3.1: *The macro-prudential and micro-prudential perspectives compared*

Source: Borio (2003)

Perhaps the best profile of macro-prudential policy to regulation (as opposed to the traditional micro) is the approach developed in recent years by the Bank for International Settlements (BIS) and summarised in Table 3.1.

In brief, the micro approach as practiced currently evaluates risks posed by individual institutions from a bottom-up standpoint, while the macro one is a top-down analysis focused on system-wide risk.

Early implementation steps

WHILE BANK REGULATORS acknowledge that they are just beginning to agree the initiatives which will shape the future of global regulation, one can summarise several of the more important announcements made at the time of writing in early 2010.

- The Financial Stability Board has moved to achieve the targets set for it by the G20 leaders. A peer review of bank compensation practices is to be completed by March 2010.
- EU finance ministers in December 2009 agreed the creation of three new watchdogs (in Paris, London and Frankfurt) to provide more centralised, pan-European oversight, and a new European Systemic Risk Board will monitor systemic risks in the EU.
- The Basel Committee on Banking Supervision (via its Cross-Border Bank Resolution Group) has issued a number of recommendations regarding national resolution powers.
- The US Federal Reserve Board, according to Chairman Ben Bernanke, is "Expanding our cross-firm, or horizontal, reviews of large institutions ... creating an enhanced quantitative supervision surveillance programme ... in sum, taking a more proactive and comprehensive approach to oversight."

This completes the introductory chapters which set the stage for our interview process and results. The following three chapters examine each of what we regard the key differentiators of bank regulators around the world.

Chapter 4: Regulatory structure and policy

"Risk control is very complex. We know banks will find a way to shift risk elsewhere. We're playing with fire, and we've only just started!" (Member of the Committee of European Bank Supervisors)

"Whatever your structure or rules, most of them failed [during the crisis]." (Clive Briault, former FSA executive)

A COUNTRY'S REGULATORY STRUCTURE AND POLICY comprise one of the most obvious differentiators which could determine its relative success in dealing with the type of issues which bedevilled the global banking system in 2007–8. A multitude of factors drive a country's regulatory structure and policy: past history, in particular of banking crises; the structure, sophistication and risk preference of the banking system; the character of governance in the country, and the reputation of key personalities in the system.

Structural issues in a diverse environment

THIS DIVERSITY RAISES A NUMBER OF QUESTIONS. Is there an ideal structure? Is one regulator the answer, or is the so-called tripartite arrangement with the central bank, dedicated supervisor and finance ministry equally or more effective? Should an independent supervisory authority be spun off from the central bank? What evidence is there of outperformance of any one structure against peer approaches? Are there overlaps or gaps which impair performance? Regulation and supervision are widely viewed as two sides of the same coin, but is one more effective than the other in a particular structure? In the debate between a principles-based or rules-based philosophy, is one approach preferable over the other?

The literature on bank regulatory structures and policies does not provide much assistance in addressing these questions. Perhaps the leading contributor to the available literature is Professor James Barth (a key US government advisor and Lowder Eminent Scholar in Finance at Auburn University and a Senior Fellow at the Milken Institute whose research focuses on financial institutions and capital markets) whose surveys in recent years of virtually all banking systems in the world provide a glimpse of the relative importance of the different structural choices. Some of his data is provided below.

The following are the major themes raised in our interview series on the topic of structure and policy:

- The role of the central bank;
- Gaps and overlaps in bank regulation:
- The importance of communication and collaboration in a multiple regulatory structure;
- Principles-based vs. rules-based policy: is there a fundamental difference?
- The balance between regulation and supervision;
- Has one particular structure clearly outperformed the others?

Role of the central bank

THE LATEST SUCH SURVEY of regulatory structures, carried out by Professor Barth in 2006, highlights the relative importance of the country's central bank in the structure. In 90, or 59% of the 152 countries surveyed, the central bank is either the sole banking regulator or shares the responsibility with one or more others, such as the finance ministry or a stand-alone bank regulator. Figure 4.1 provides pie charts for the category of developed markets indicating that the central bank in 47% of the cases supervises banks, in 37% of the countries a single financial supervisory agency has that role, while in 11% of the markets there are multiple banking supervisory agencies.

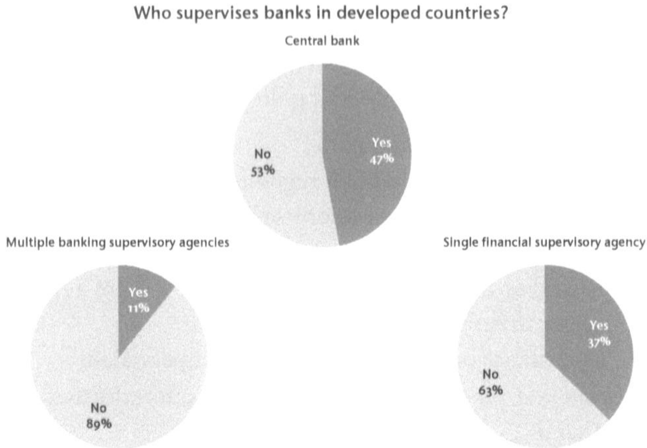

Figure 4.1: *Bank supervision structures*

Source: James R. Barth, Auburn University and Milken Institute

In his evaluation of relative performance, Professor Barth concludes that more regulation – in whatever structure – correlates negatively with systemic performance, largely due to the corruption which may accompany a strong regulatory influence. Interestingly, in none of our interviews – admittedly in developed markets – was corruption mentioned as an issue.

Figure 4.2 provides a useful diagram for the institutional setting of bank regulation, indicating, among other things, how political influence and corruption can influence bank regulation and supervision. We shall return to this topic of political influence in Chapter 6.

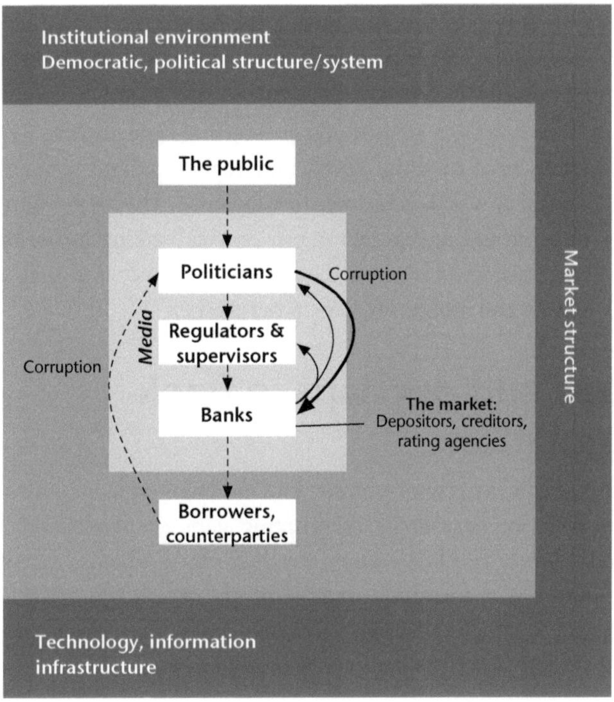

Figure 4.2: *A framework for understanding bank regulation and supervision*

Source: Barth, James R., Gerard Caprio, Jr., and Ross Levine, *Rethinking Bank Regulation: Till Angels Govern*, CUP (2008)

Given the greater focus as indicated in the previous chapter on systemic, or macro-prudential supervision, many observers believe that the central bank, especially one with a successful macro-economic track record in managing money supply and interest rates, is a logical choice to manage, or at least to share the management of, the bank regulatory system. In both the UK and US, which have suffered particularly from the crisis, a public debate on this issue is commanding the headlines.

A very senior UK banker reflects on the merits of combining macro-economic and macro-prudential regulation:

> "It's a good way to go if you are starting from scratch. Regulators need to think about new regulation and prudential capital as well as customer relationships. The ideal might be to bring all this together in one central banking authority. If not, you could hive off the consumer agency and keep the macro and institutional aspects together."

Gaps and overlaps in bank regulation

REGULATORY SYSTEMS OFTEN ARE SHAPED over a period of years without necessarily eliminating gaps or overlaps in responsibilities. The US system, the history of which is profiled in Figure 4.3, is a leading example of one which has evolved in response to crises and other external events but without ensuring a smooth interface between its components.

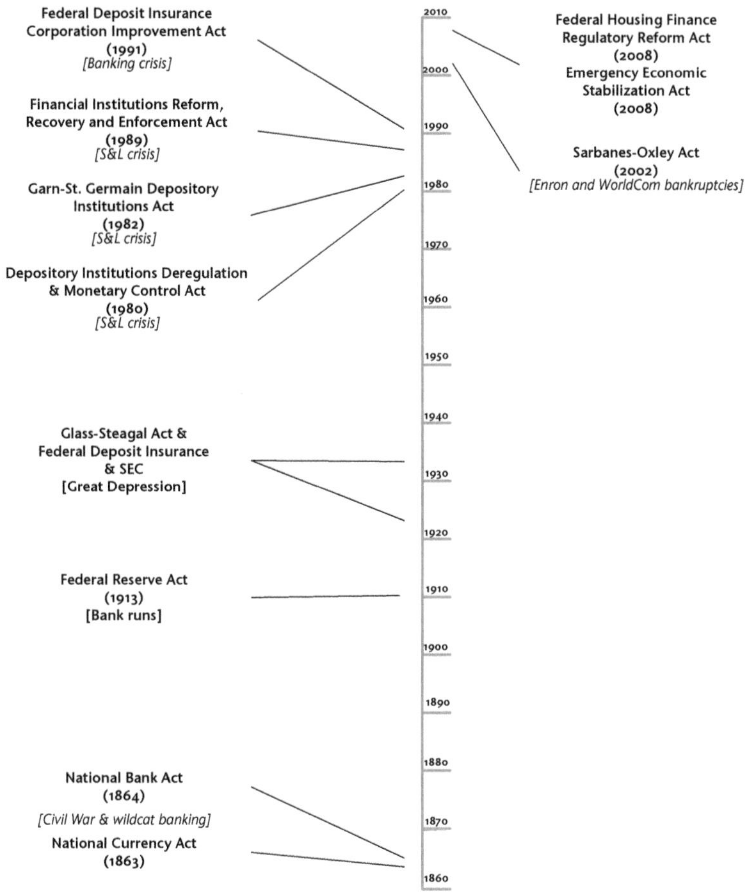

Figure 4.3: *Impact of crises on US bank regulation*

Source: Barth, James R., et al, *The Rise and Fall of the US Mortgage and Credit Markets: A Comprehensive Analysis of the Market Meltdown*, John Wiley & Sons (2009)

Our interviewees were particularly harsh on the US structure. As the CEO of a major US bank explained:

> "We have four agencies embedded in our bank. Shrinking their number isn't even on the table. The US regulatory system is old and antiquated, with the worst mortgage system on the planet. Multiple regulators are a big problem, and we're doing nothing to reduce them. We'll create a committee of regulators, with a 'systemic' regulator at the head. It's not optimal but it's OK."

His views are echoed by the executive in another leading US bank with responsibility for regulatory relationships:

> "There are gaps in the remits (responsibilities) which are no fault of the regulators involved. A lot falls between the cracks. The Fed didn't use the powers it was given, such as mortgage origination, where they could have been much more aggressive. It all goes back to the implementation of Basel II, which required the US investment banks to have a consolidated regulator. The US investment banks needed one in the US, and it was decided that the Securities and Exchange Commission (SEC) would be selected."

A veteran US bank analyst, Robert Albertson, Chief Strategist at Sandler O'Neill, comments on the suitability of the SEC, which essentially focuses on regulating the markets, as a supervisor of the US banks:

> "Look back at the 1980s: the banking system got overtaken by the securities markets; the shadow banking system dominates the mortgage market. The SEC should have understood these markets far better. The problem is that they sit in the weeds, preferring to be 'precisely wrong' rather than approximately right –marking to market became too narrow and myopic'!"

A senior European central banking official concurs:

"The US was a disaster waiting to happen – especially the securitisation problem and weak monitoring – despite embedded supervisors. We assumed they were informed on risk. Our suspicions were correct; they 'didn't want to interfere'. Perhaps the worst example of bad supervision during the crisis!"

Andy Maguire, London-based partner for banking of consultants Boston Consulting Group, emphasises a generic point made by others:

"Multiple regulators will always be more trouble. Each will have his own rules and responses. They won't want to do the other's job for them."

Communication and collaboration – critical success factors

ALL OF OUR INTERVIEWEES AGREED that, in a multiple regulatory structure, effective communication and collaboration are critical success factors. This unsurprising conclusion is particularly relevant in a banking crisis which demands action. Two success stories in particular are cited by our interviewees.

Ted Price of the Office of Supervision of Financial Institutions (OSFI) in Canada, widely cited as one of the most effective regulators during the crisis, points out that:

"Co-operation across Federal financial regulatory agencies in Canada is extremely close. A number of round tables related to financial services exist: FISC (which is chaired by the Superintendent of Financial Institutions (OSFI), and includes the Bank of Canada, the Department of Finance, the Canada Deposit Insurance Corporation and the Financial Consumer Agency of Canada.) Another is SAC – which includes the same agencies as FISC, but is headed by the Department of Finance, as well as CEIC which brings together the top 5-10 key players in financial institution regulation. We all work together on oversight, but each has very specific mandates that rarely overlap. This worked, in part because of our mandates; but also because there is a shared interest in keeping the Canadian financial system strong."

A similar story is told by Bjørn Skogstad Aamo, a career civil servant running Norway's highly regarded Finanstylsinet, the country's financial supervisory agency:

> "We call ourselves supervisors in a tripartite relationship (with the central bank and the finance ministry). It helps to be a small country; people went to university together. We have a close and open co-operation. All supervisory reports are made available to the central bank. They act on issues of macro stability; in our view they can be too harsh or lenient, but it's the basis for the tripartite relationship – there are no secrets."

The Commission Bancaire's former executive Jean-Louis Fort summarises the views of many of his peers in an integrated structure:

> "Being part of the central bank provides rigour and confidence in the dialogue with the banks, which enables you to influence their culture."

In contrast to these success stories, there is the experience in the US and UK. One of our interviewees notes that in "global terms, the UK and US bankers were engaged in a race to the bottom."

Those who have read 'Too Big to Fail', the story of the collaboration in the US between the Fed's Ben Bernanke and Tim Geithner and the Treasury's Henry Paulson can have little doubt about the value of their collaboration in 2008 before and after the Lehman collapse in 2008.

A senior UK banker notes that:

> "The working relationship between the FSA and other regulators has not been what it should have been! There should be close, strong and senior relationships between banks and their regulators, backed by authority. It would have made a difference! In the UK, it was clear that Royal Bank of Scotland (RBS) was overstretched; RBS was the defining element of the crisis in the UK."

Principles-based vs. rules-based policy: is there a fundamental difference?

ONE OF THE QUESTIONS frequently cited as central to a regulator's policy doctrine is the distinction between one that is principles-based – i.e. based on a limited number of basic principles such as capital adequacy or adequate liquidity – and one of rules, or specific targets or limits such as the Tier 1 ratio. Both rules-based and principles-based approaches suffered; the SEC's rules-based approach in the US and the FSA's principles-based one in the UK, among other markets.

Many of our interviewees took a different approach to the matter.

For Lucas van Praag of Goldman Sachs, the issue is results:

> "Rules-based regulation doesn't work very well; banks are very adept at finding ways around them. Consider structured investment vehicles, or SIVs, and other off balance sheet vehicles. These were perfectly legal, but hid the true risks banks were exposed to. In principles-based regulation, the onus is on the regulated entity. What's more important is the spirit and intent of regulation."

Stefan Gavell of State Street Bank agrees:

"The important distinction is between prudential and other roles. Under prudential, one evaluates not just the rules but also the effect on the economy, such as knock-on effects in a broader context. Thus a prudential regulator can impose restrictions as an interpreter of the markets – such as the Fed's role in limiting lending to commercial real estate; a more broadly based approach than, for example, that of the SEC."

The balance between regulation and supervision

MAKING THE RULES (i.e. regulation) is clearly conceptually different from enforcing them – the supervision function. Many bank regulators thus have separate but parallel functions in their organisation chart. One of them, the highly regarded Bank of Spain, praises the virtues of 'four eyes' – two separate points of view which examine each issue or decision through extensive discussion and collaboration.

But the relative performance of each can vary widely, and the evolving debate over macro-prudential or systemic regulation poses new challenges.

In the EU, where the 27 national regulators have begun to bring together their respective policies in the context of guidelines to be issued by the Committee of European Banking Supervisors (CEBS), the challenge is particularly acute.

One of these senior regulators describes the challenge:

"The issue of regulation vs. supervision is the big question. What is the role of supervision in the future? You can be a good regulator and a bad supervisor. All this relates to the question of macro supervision. You must distinguish between policy, regulation and supervision. You need both rules and supervisory discretion, but we're not there yet! We need to be transparent on Pillar 2, but the question is how much discretion to allow? Macro policy and regulation will need to cover supervision as well. We can agree on a few rules, like linking the capital buffer with expected loss, or a minimum 8% capital ratio, or an additional macro buffer which can be released in bad times. But risk control is very complex, and we know banks will complain about the level playing field and will find a way to shift risk elsewhere. We're playing with fire! No one in Europe really had macro supervision in the past. I live with this! And we're only starting to work on it!"

Is there a single best regulatory structure?

OUR INTERVIEWEES ARE VIRTUALLY UNANIMOUS in their agreement: no one structure is clearly superior.

From the academic standpoint, Professor James Barth points out that:

> "There's no evidence that one structure is better than another; both the US and UK models have had problems. Consolidating agencies is a good idea if only for cost reduction, but there's lots of pressure to preserve jobs and power."

Management consultant Dominik Treeck of Oliver Wyman concurs:

> "Regulatory structure is not a sufficient differentiator."

A senior UK regulator agrees on the basis of relative success:

> "There's no single winner. Canada has a separate supervisor, Spain combines it all in one agency. But both did well."

Perhaps the best summary on structure is offered by Clive Briault, the former head of retail supervision at the FSA in London:

"The crisis affected equally both single and multiple regulatory jurisdictions. The key to success is to spot big risks and address them. The crisis was a collective intellectual failure, and regulators were part of it. Whatever your structure or rules, most of them failed. Regulation is no good if you're looking at the wrong crisis."

Chapter 5: The role of professional skills

"The big issue: it's the mindset of the supervisor."
(David Llewellyn, Professor of Money and Banking, Loughborough University, Honorary Visiting Professor, Cass Business School)

Searching finance

THIS CHAPTER RECORDS OUR INTERVIEWEES' VIEWS in response to a general question about the adequacy of the skills needed to achieve their agency's objectives: leadership, availability, challenges, limitations, and career paths. They place a particular focus on the skills required in the two key roles of regulator and supervisor. Their key issues include:

- The central role of leadership;
- The unique challenges of regulation and supervision;
- Attracting and retaining qualified key professionals;
- The roles of the regulator and supervisor;
- Building a career path in a regulatory team; and
- Challenges for the future.

The central role of leadership

AS IN SO MANY OTHER BUSINESSES, the adequacy of leadership is the focus of many views expressed. Professor James Barth notes that:

> "Problems are at the top of the agencies – the people who have to make decisions. They could have done better. You need to hold people accountable if they make mistakes. A risk expert can get hired away, but you don't need a PhD to see that 100% finance is risky!"

Sandler O'Neill's Principal Chief Strategist and leading bank analyst Robert Albertson adds:

> "You must have leadership skills and know how to manage: to go into a bank and say 'you may be right, but I want you to take your projections back and use this wider range of assumptions'. In short, to consider true stress scenarios, not fostering denial! The problem is at several levels: not just strong bankers but also regulators with strong backbones."

The US regulatory structure has attracted considerable criticism as well as proposed solutions. For Bob Kelly, CEO of BNY Mellon:

> "It's not rocket science. It's a management issue, not structure, and it starts at the top."

Another US banker agrees:

> "The challenge in regulation is not so much about people. By and large the quality of supervisors has improved enormously in recent years. You can hire people who believe strongly in what they do and are comfortable with current levels of compensation. The challenge is more about objectives and tools of supervision."

The unique challenges of regulation and supervision

Compensation

MANY OBSERVERS POINT to the unique challenges faced by regulators. One is compensation, in particular for the highly skilled individuals who could pursue a banking career. Roberto Violi of the Banca d'Italia summarises a common view:

> "It's a very difficult problem for the future: how to recruit talent? You must pay decently. It's an issue that has been placed under the carpet. A supervisor may be paid one-tenth of that received by the bank executive he supervises. If you're concerned about quality, you have to pay more. Supervisors are not standard bureaucrats."

Regulatory capture

A RELATED ISSUE is so-called 'regulatory capture': a supervisor who does not stand up for his/her own views or simply parrots those of the bank he/she supervises. In many cases the person accepts a job with the regulated institution, thus depriving the regulator of talent and experience.

Thus a London-based management consultant notes that:

> "There's little value in embedded regulators in US banks like Citibank – look at all the mistakes made. Banks have captured regulators. How do you make a regulatory career more attractive? Don't rely on rotation into and out of the private sector: it's too cosy."

A senior financial regulator agrees:

> "The US regulatory agencies deploy a 'masses of asses' approach to supervision: this is a tragic waste. Take a lot of good people, put them on-site, and sit back and watch the regulatory capture. You don't want people liking or needing their regulated institution and the people that work there, but the US approach really risks this outcome. It's better to keep both physical and emotional differences: go on-site for visits, for sure, but don't live there."

Political pressure

FINALLY, REGULATORS CAN be put under massive political pressure, particularly in the US. A senior US banker with extensive dealings with a number of US regulators points out that:

> "In the US, if you don't like something you go to your congressman or senator. That puts the heat on regulators. It's the US system of checks and balances; you lean on regulators."

Attracting and retaining qualified key professionals

THE CHALLENGES CURRENTLY FACED by regulators are daunting. Attracting and retaining the unique skill sets needed are equally challenging. A senior FSA executive summarises them well for an agency such as his:

> 'What are we asking of supervisors? A combination of many qualities: access to credit officers, country credit expertise, deep knowledge of banking and finance, economic evaluation, and the big role: the ability to be convincing to senior officers in banks. It's a universal problem – squaring the circle of being outside the bank yet understanding the inside. Someone who has the overall vision as to what are the most central issues – the messages to leave with management. And on top of all that you have a competitive market!"

His former colleague Michael Foot, a career regulator with the Bank of England and the FSA and now of Promontory Capital Group (UK), balances the risks and rewards:

> 'You can earn more for less in the private sector. The benefits of being a regulator are less than the costs – including the grief you get! It takes a very dedicated public servant. Some are committed, but there's always a problem of balancing risks and rewards. People can do a cost/benefit analysis!'

Management consultant Dominik Treeck, Senior Manager at Oliver Wyman in Washington DC, who has extensive experience in working with bank regulators, reinforces the point:

> "To develop regulation, you need individuals with broad knowledge and a passion for the subject. Examiners play a different role – and they have probably been one of the main soft spots of the system. You need people with in-depth operational understanding of the institutions they supervise as

well as a broader perspective on industry trends, e.g. with respect to product development. Many regulatory bodies are struggling with this question: how are we going to get quality supervisors?"

Roles of the regulator and supervisor

THE CRITICAL SUCCESS FACTORS for the regulator differ from that of the supervisor. For the former, a reputation for independence of judgement, macro-economic track record and insight into banking issues are most prized. The ECB's head, Jean-Claude Trichet, is often held up as a role model, while Ben Bernanke of the Fed is highly respected for his judgment, independence and communication skills. Thus a senior executive of a major US investment bank is:

> "... extraordinarily impressed with the Fed as its new regulator. Even though it was embedded in the firm, the SEC (his former regulator) is essentially an investor protection agency; they weren't supposed to be a bank regulator! Fed people are informed, thoughtful and not hesitant about asking questions."

The chairman of a major global bank agrees:

> "In the US, our experience with the OCC [Office of the Comptroller of the Currency] and Fed has not been bad; the guy from the Fed didn't miss a trick!"

In Asia, a regional Fitch executive cites the high calibre of Hong Kong and Singapore regulators.

> "In Asia they need to be impartial and respected, and they have high calibre staff that understand risk and can communicate their views to banks."

At the top end of the regulatory spectrum are those who deal with the largest and most complex firms. As BCG's Andy Maguire notes:

> "At the top end, people are everything. Banks like Goldman Sachs are good at risk and you need supervisors who are the best – high quality."

Our interviewees agreed on the role played by most supervisory professionals, whether embedded or relying on site visits.

Former FSA executive Clive Briault notes that:

> "Supervisors are people who monitor whether regulated firms are meeting both high-level principles and more detailed rules. The key is how supervisors do their job; is it top down or bottom up?"

The Banca de España in Madrid is cited by many of our sources as a highly professional organisation. A senior supervisor there, who manages teams embedded in the major banks, explains that:

> "We have some 30 supervisors in Santander, but they're not talking to the CEO but rather doing detailed analysis, loan by loan, based on the credit register."

The CEO of a major Spanish bank summarises his positive views of local supervisors:

> "The quality of supervisors has improved dramatically in Spain: they can understand and deal with the actual situation, not just apply rules. Most are technocrats by career, and switch teams to prevent undue relationships with a single bank. They're good technicians and know their job, but perhaps aren't creative. They tend to be hierarchical and ruled by rules. If there's an exception, they have to go up the organisation. The response often is 'we understand, but the rules say ...'."

Building a career path in a regulatory team

NOT SURPRISINGLY, SOME OF THE MOST SUCCESSFUL AGENCIES have developed career paths which address both the quality and retention issues discussed above. In many countries, the central bank or finance ministry can attract the best and brightest talent interested in a public sector career. In contrast, a separate supervisory agency like the FSA may lose talent to the private sector.

The highly regarded OSFI in Canada attributes the close co-operation of its Federal bank deregulatory agencies to such a common background, as the OFSI's Ted Price comments:

> "Co-operation across Federal financial regulatory agencies in Canada is extremely close, in part because of our mandates, but also because there is a shared interest in keeping the Canadian financial system strong.. There is also a strong relationship between regulators as many employees have worked at the other agencies, which helps produce a shared sense of purpose."

Bjørn Skogstad Aamo, head of Norway's Financial Supervisory Authority, reinforces the point. He is a former Undersecretary of the Ministry of Finance and head of the Prime Minister's office during the 1990s banking crisis.

> "Most Norwegian inspectors have been career bankers. We recruit those with 10-15 years' experience; they know the industry and are in their 40s and may make a career choice. They may feel pressure in the bank to sell and want to do something different to maintain their professional standards. They may get paid less, but better than most civil servants. It creates a virtuous circle – only a few were doing this at the beginning, but other former bankers have been attracted to it as an accepted second career."

Challenges for the future

Getting a balanced skill set

A COMMON VIEW of our interviewees is that skills *between* those traditionally found in bank regulators and supervisors – neither a macro theoretician as in a central bank nor a processor/auditor ticking boxes as a supervisor – will be needed in the future. Thus a senior German banker dealing with their regulators believes that:

> "At the top of the Bundesbank people are very bright but lack banking experience. At BaFin they struggle with the complexity of regulation and get lost in the detail. The rules are too complex. Regulators need better staff – to upskill for the whole sector. How do you really understand the issues? You need detailed knowledge of what happens in a bank. Most don't understand the boxes they tick."

This view is echoed by one of the 27 heads of national regulators making up the CEBS in Brussels.

> "The issue of regulation vs. supervision is the right one. What are their roles? Perhaps a balance of the two. All this relates to the question of the future of macro supervision. More complex regulation means more likelihood of capture! Central banking people are very macro with a helicopter view: some really don't know what a bank is! Supervisors are at the micro level to implement rules. It's very much an audit culture and compliance with regulations. Banks are very complex organisations and the supervisors end up with a compliance role. And they are very busy at it! Banks find a way to shift risk elsewhere, but regulators don't have that kind of instinct; we should have people to answer questions like 'if we regulators do this, what do you bankers do?' The

big question therefore is how to organise the regulatory structure. But you need both macro and micro!"

Chapter 6: Politics and bank regulation

"Nothing creates better supervision than a major failure"
(Charles Littrell, APRA)

Searching finance

EVEN THE MOST CASUAL READER of the general press in the wake of the recent banking crisis is aware of the interest – if not anger – of the man in the street over what would be in normal circumstances arcane financial issues. Television coverage in the US of Fed Chairman Ben Bernanke being arraigned in 'town meetings' over the failure of banks and regulators and its impact on the voters' net worth and job prospects is an example, albeit fairly unique on a global scale, of how voters can sway decisions on regulatory matters.

This chapter will thus address the last of the three important drivers of relative success or failure of bank regulation and supervision. It will focus on such variables as the relative trust of the voters in the regulatory authorities, the history of local bank regulation and past banking crises, and banking structures which may lead to an intensification of the political debate. It will provide some detail on the political issues in three different markets – the US, Spain and Germany – in which the political debate has played a major influence in shaping bank regulation.

Drivers of political influence

THE REGULATION OF BANKING is a universal phenomenon, yet it captures the headlines in some countries rather than others. What drives this relative importance of political influence? Some of the factors include:

- **The presence of segments of the banking sector with particularly strong influence on the political debate.** In democracies such as the US, Spain and Germany, legislative elections are often shaped by banks able to finance and otherwise influence the votes of their legislators. Thus the case studies of community banks in the US and savings banks in Germany and Spain are provided below as an example of such influence.

- **A history of past banking problems and the positive role of regulators in addressing them.** A number of our interviewees in markets such as Australia, Norway, Canada, and Brazil pointed to their banking or economic crises which occurred in living memory – usually of the 1990s – which have produced regulatory regimes which are widely respected by voters and the political forces. In Chapter 7, we profile case studies of APRA in Australia, OSFI in Canada, the Banque de France, the Banca d'Italia and the Financial Supervision Authority in Norway. In a word, in these countries, as well as others not profiled, there is a relatively high degree of trust in the bank regulator.
- **A liberal political and economic philosophy, as opposed to a top-down, command and control approach.** Thus the decisions of bank regulators in countries like China and Russia, where the government effectively dictates banking regulation as well as other key policies, are rarely the object of open political debate. We were not encouraged to include such regulators in our survey!

In Chapter 7, we profile a number of national case studies of bank regulation. Below we examine three of these markets in which political factors have played a particularly strong role in shaping the regulatory dialogue.

The United States

BELOW THE HANDFUL OF MAJOR BANKS like Citibank which dominate the headlines are roughly 8,000 smaller so-called community banks, which are deeply embedded in their local community. They are generally regulated by state authorities and tend to have close and powerful relationships with these local legislators. They have little interest in becoming regulated by the major Federal institutions such as the OCC and Federal Reserve.

A senior banker at Citibank expresses a common view on the power of smaller, community banks in the political debate:

> "There's a difference between big banks and community ones. The latter are closer to congressmen and senators, which is where the power lies. There's limited appetite for change; it's the US banking system in action."

Another veteran US banker with responsibility for regulatory relationships points up the Federal Reserve as a political target:

> "The Fed has a lead role in systemic regulation but is very unpopular; the view is that the Fed should lose something. The man in the street wants some people to go to jail. You need a master of the issues (like Mr. Bernanke) but also show people that you have a cop on the beat!"

A leading US bank strategist in NY expresses a highly emotional but typical view:

> "Politicians have lost all sophistication. I've never seen it sink to this level – sheer meanness. It's a food fight for votes – populism on the line. Geithner [at Treasury] and the regulators in 2008 did the best they could. Look at the record of political appointees going way back. The percentage from the private sector has varied between 29–58%; under Obama, it's only 8%. It's a shame! The US community banks themselves are vulnerable [to regulatory action] with their problem commercial real estate portfolios."

> A retired regional bank CEO is more specific about the problem:

> "It's MONEY! Congressmen need to run for re-election, the cost of campaigning has skyrocketed, and serving Con-

gressmen need to get funded. Why is it so hard to regulate financial institutions? Maybe it will happen!"

A US bank CEO ranks the agencies which regulate his bank as an indication of the problem:

"If the Fed is B to B-plus..., our state regulator is C minus."

Spain

Another form of political influence from a sector of the banking system is the role of the Spanish *cajas*, or savings banks. Representing perhaps half of the country's total banking assets, their market share until the banking crisis had steadily increased as they took ground from the commercial banks. Local politicians exercise considerable influence on the banks' governance. Now they are in disarray, as their exposure to problem real estate loans has brought a warning from the central bank that the sector must consolidate.

A Spanish bank CEO interviewed for this book sets out the problem:

"It's a political issue. The Banca de España has argued for independence like the US Fed, but they don't have the political clout as regional banks have their own powers over the 50–60 local *cajas*. It isn't as much involved in the *cajas*. The Banca de España has been crying wolf about real estate concentration since 2005, sending a message to the market. But local politicians aren't interested in messages when home owners' interests are involved! Political groups get in the way; they oppose legislation for mergers."

Andy Maguire of BCG puts it more succinctly:

"The Banca de España can't control the *cajas*."

On the other hand, a US banker graphically describes the political challenge:

"What if same regulator went to the prime minister and said 'this practice is very risky; we want to do something like lower loan to value ratios or increase the capital buffer.' Would the regulator be able to count on the government's support for potentially unpopular measures?"

Germany

A similar situation to the Spanish model exists in Germany, where savings banks dominate local banking markets. The regulatory threat they pose is an indirect one via their ownership of the *Landesbanken* – regional banks whose traditional role has been to act as central bankers to their savings bank owners. In recent years *Landesbanken* have been active lenders to marginal borrowers on a global scale, with real estate concentration a typical problem. While *Landesbanken* such as West LB have suffered a severe impairment of capital on several occasions in the past few decades, their owners have generally restored the capital base.

A veteran German senior banker expresses a common view:

"*Landesbanken* have lousy corporate governance; ex-politicians run the savings banks. BaFin concentrates on it, and the intensity of the dialogue has increased; it won't go away! BaFin can't tell them what model to use; it's not BaFin's role."

BaFin head Jochen Sanio confirms his frustration:

"We aren't blind! The *Landesbanken* have had problems with their business model, especially with respect to their size. *Landesbanken* were able to try lots of business models as long as they had sufficient capital and their owners could dig deep into their own pockets to add more as required. At this moment it is hard to say whether they will be successful in adapting their business model to the changes taking place in the financial markets. That's the fundamental problem which has to be resolved. In the past, BaFin could only act when a bank's untenable strategy had come completely unstuck and ended in failure. The better way forward is to follow the old motto 'prevention is better than cure'. Before the crisis there was no legal basis for us to prohibit specific business or takeover activities by our banks as long as they did not reveal severe deficiencies in their internal organisation. In other words, we were rather powerless when confronted with weak and risky business models. Recent amendments to the German Banking Act which came into force in mid-2009 enable us to step in much earlier now.

"In the deregulatory environment of the past, 'market discipline' rather than strict regulation was deemed to be the most efficient tool in constraining banks' risk-taking. This approach has failed miserably. The crisis has finally broken the unsound theory of market discipline beyond repair. It did not stand the real test in the real world."

Further observations

Regulator strength

Our interviewees focused on regulator backbone as a critical success factor in resisting political influence. In this respect, Oliver Wyman consultant Dominik Treeck's prize goes to the European Central Bank (ECB):

"One role model for macro prudential regulation is the ECB. For historical and institutional reasons, Mr. Trichet and his board are able to resist political pressures. They have proven backbone when the public demands lower interest rates and he hears from Mr. Sarkozy and Mrs. Merkel."

Former FSA regulator Clive Briault agrees:

> "Look at the political climate in the early 2000s. In many countries it was unrealistic at the time to expect a bank regulator to stand up and imply that home ownership should be restricted or that tax incentives to purchase property and to take out debt should be removed."

Asia

Asian banks so far have succeeded in minimising political pressure. As a Fitch executive in Asia points out, banks in his region have performed much better than was the case in the Asian crisis of 1997, in part at least due to improved regulation. He notes that:

> "In Hong Kong and Singapore, bank regulators are impartial and highly respected; they have high calibre staff that understand risk and communicate their views to the banks. In other markets like the Philippines, it's more difficult, given the power of business dynasties that control many banks."

Government support

Are there other indicators of success in resisting political pressure? One suggested to us is that the presence of a small number of large banks is a positive factor, based largely on the success of the Australian and Canadian bank regulators. This may be true, but it doesn't help those regulators that have a plethora of smaller banks as do those in the US, Spain and Germany.

Perhaps the final thought on this issue goes to one of the more successful regulators:

> "In the long run, prudential supervision is a function of government support. The huge difference is in political and supervisory culture .... In the US, the Fed and OCC have

some of the smartest and most committed supervisors in the world, but the lack of political backing guaranteed that eventually disaster would strike … . When politicians love bankers and resent supervisors, taxpayers should get out their wallets, because the bailout is coming!"

Chapter 7: Regulatory authority case studies

"The critical success factors for bank regulation are: leadership and experience; an apolitical environment; up-to-date understanding of the the business; and avoiding unintended consequences"
(Robert Albertson, Chief Strategist, Sandler O'Neill)

Introduction

THIS CHAPTER IS BUILT around a single question asked of each interviewee: which regulators in your view have had a particularly successful or unsuccessful experience in addressing the issues during the recent financial crisis? The purpose, as stated in Chapter 1, was to identify lessons which might be useful in mitigating future crises.

Having thus identified such regulators, we asked them, as well as our other sources, what lessons they drew from the experience. The first part of this chapter therefore contains the case studies. In most cases, our findings are derived from two sources:

1 The profile and structure as provided from websites and published material as well as insights from interviews with the agency's management; and
2 Comments from other interviewees to provide some independent perspective.

The chapter concludes with our observations from an analysis of this material. Specifically, what conclusions can be drawn from the relative success or failure of the particular agency analysed? Are there any lessons which might be relevant to other regulators? Can one conclude from the evidence that a given regulator is a clear case study of success or failure, or are there other, external drivers of this outcome?

Australia: Australian Prudential Regulatory Authority (APRA)

Profile

ESTABLISHED IN 1998, APRA has responsibility in Australia for regulating all deposit-taking institutions, life and non-life insurers, and superannuation (pension) funds.

Its single purpose is to ensure the prudent behaviour of financial institutions, and its vision is to be 'a world-class prudential supervisor recognised for its leadership, professionalism and innovation'. Australia has adopted the 'twin peaks' structure in which APRA works closely with the country's central bank, the Reserve Bank of Australia (RBA). The four dominant banks regulated by APRA – National Bank of Australia, Westpac, CBA and the ANZ – comprise the 'four pillars' within which mergers are not permitted as a matter of national policy.

Australia has navigated the 2007–09 financial crisis quite successfully, a view which has been confirmed by our interviewees. The banks had only minimum exposure to sub-prime and structured products, and non-performing loans in general have been below the level during the difficult period during the 1990s, which led to the formation of APRA. The leading banks continue to report double-digit ROEs despite the crisis.

The agency adopted a policy of stress-testing the banks' housing loans before the recent crisis, with increased intensity of supervision; some 570 prudential conversations took place during a recent 12-month period. Teams of supervisors and risk management specialists have carried out visits across the system as well as thematic analysis and visits with banks' boards of directors. Another priority has been the banks' remuneration practices. APRA has also been proactive in raising the quality of Tier 1 capital.

APRA recently joined the Basel Committee of Bank Supervisors. It introduced the Basel II structure in 2008.

A senior executive of APRA interviewed for this book summarises their key success factors thus:

> "What are the key success factors in regulation? For us, they include:
>
> - A proactive supervisory culture in the good times; prudential supervision is most valuable when it is least valued. An example is the joint approach taken by APRA and the RBA when we identified very worrisome trends in home prices and home loan growth in 2001–02. The RBA started jawboning; we started tightening both regulation and supervision. On the supervision front we conducted a stress test in 2002–03 in which the Loss Given Default (LGD) was 30% plus expenses and Probability of Default (PD) about 20 times worse that anything historically experienced across Australia, but consistent with losses in similar economies such as Texas, California and southern England. On the regulatory front we doubled the capital required for lenders' mortgage insurance companies and made the capital allocation more risk-based. We did not ban sub-prime loans, but as a supervisory matter they were effectively discouraged. We added capital for home loans which were high LTV, low doc or otherwise non-standard. The result was that, what was an over-heating home loan market moderated, and the Australian house price bubble deflated slowly from 2003 through 2007, and home loan losses were very small.
> - Having a good relationship with the central bank is very useful. Most countries with independent supervisors have central banks which want to second-guess

the supervisor; we are fortunate in our case that the original APRA staff were transferred from the RBA bank supervision department, and the RBA and APRA work closely and effectively together.

- It is important as a supervisory matter to work with boards, where possible. Our regulation and supervision seeks to empower and inform boards, so that they have some hope of moderating risky behaviour by their management teams.
- The ability to set individual capital requirements, and the ability to issue statutory direction, are both very useful. For example, we hold conversations with bank boards where we say, 'Here are some examples of your risk management shortcomings. Until we feel that you are taking these issues seriously, your capital requirement is 10%, not 8%'. "

Other perspectives

When asked about APRA's success, interestingly, most of our interviewees pointed not to these qualities but rather general factors such as the concentrated structure of the Australian banking system, the economy's export success, and the impact of the earlier economic crisis.

A little-noticed variable is the funding problem faced during the recent financial crisis, when the Australian government guaranteed bank borrowings abroad to facilitate its banks' funding needs.

Our APRA interviewee, referring to this development, noted:

> "We don't always get it right in time. Our next big project in 2007 was going to be tightening up the liquidity rules, but the market beat us to the punch!"

Again, a Fitch Asian executive provides a rating agency's overall perspective:

> "They are pretty clued up in Australia, and the regulators are getting a fair amount of praise. Banks have done well. Some of that may be due to APRA, but is it just a matter of luck? There are no party politics in Australia, and the banking system is dominated by four local banks – not a lot of intermediaries. So was it structure or APRA? The offshore borrowing of Australian banks was a weakness."

Canada: Office of the Superintendent of Financial Institutions (OSFI)

Profile

ESTABLISHED IN 1987, Canada's single financial regulator has responsibility, reporting to the finance ministry, for all Canadian banks as well as insurers, pension funds and other financial institutions. The success of the country's major banks in navigating the recent financial crisis has attracted to OSFI the attention of banks and regulators around the world, particularly in Canada's neighbour to the south, in search of best practice in proactive and comprehensive bank regulation and supervision.

Within the agency's organisational structure, separate units are responsible for regulation and for supervision.

The regulatory framework established well before the crisis resembles in many respects that recommended today by leading bodies such as the Basel Committee and the Council of European Bank Regulators. Canada's Tier 1 minimum of 7% considerably exceeds the Basel minimum of 4%, and in addition at least 75% of this figure must be common equity. In addition, a leverage ratio – total assets divided by total capital – of 5% is in line with the targets now under consideration by regulators globally. Finally, Canadian banks with net exposure to the wholesale markets have liquidity limits for net short date exposure and must have contingency plans and stress testing liquidity measures in place.

Attention in the US has also been focused on the Canadian case study because of its regulation of the home insurance sector, which is widely regarded – particularly in the US – as the underlying cause of the recent banking crisis. Whereas in the

US there is no regulatory limit on loan-to-value ratios for home loans, those exceeding 80% in Canada must be insured for the whole amount, and total household debt service cannot legally exceed 40% of gross household income. Unlike the case in the US, where mortgage borrowers are not obliged to guarantee their mortgage loan, in Canada such a personal guarantee ensures that the borrower's other assets provide potential support.

The result has been impressive in terms of the financial performance of the leading Canadian banks. While some had significant exposure to sub-prime loans before the crisis, by 2009 this category comprised only 7% of the mortgage total against 20% in the US.

Ted Price of the OSFI attributes their success in large part to Canada's serious recession in the mid-1990s:

> "The recession in the 1990s was a wake-up call for everyone. By the early 2000s the regulatory framework had been reworked with a focus on supervision and capital levels, the banks were less leveraged, and the whole system less exposed to a crunch. When the most recent global crisis hit, Canada was thus less prone to damage. There were several factors, including luck, but both borrowers and lenders were in pretty good shape to begin with, with a higher capital base, and a leverage limit for banks which curtailed risky exposures – essentially we had a pretty conservative banking sector. Our mortgage market is also different from the US – an 80% loan to value cap and no tax deductibility for mortgage interest. Canadian banks may be somewhat conservative, but so are their borrowers, and to a certain extent, so is the regulator."

Another success factor is having one regulator for all national banks, as well as a concentrated banking system. There is extraordinarily close co-operation across the Federal agencies –

the Bank of Canada, the finance ministry, the deposit insurance scheme and the consumer protection agency.

How does OSFI's policy differ from its peers? Price points out that:

> "We're a prudential regulator, not rules-based. It works here! There's a high expectation that high quality risk management exists in OSFI. We intervene very proactively on any individual weakness of controls. There's no push-back. We have highly skilled, competent people who can assess the situation. We're an integrated regulator – both banks and insurance – so we see everything that goes on in the financial economy. And we avoid being caught up in picayune issues; we worry about the bigger ones!"

Julie Dickson, the head of OSFI, was quoted recently in the *Financial Times* on how these rules and principles are enforced in practice:

> "We want to be told everything that is going on. We don't want to have a list of boxes that we tick because that's not very effective ... The right conversation is the principle; you have to know what risks you are undertaking."

Other perspectives

Perhaps the most relevant view of OSFI comes from an individual who was most often mentioned in the same breath by other interviewees as the most successful bank regulator. This successful regulator summarises his view of OSFI:

> "The Canadians [regulators] are clearly number one; they did well despite being next to the brothel [the US]. OSFI is an industry-integrated prudential supervisor. They are very well resourced: the typical supervisor is maybe 50 years old with lots of industry experience before joining the public sector. Above all, they are proactive: they don't view them-

selves as any way subordinate to the market or the private sector. Their senior management focuses very hard on meeting with boards, chairs and CEO of big firms. Essentially, they take a personal and proactive approach and it works."

Yet once again, the multiplicity of possible success factors may well play a role in this stellar performance. A senior UK banker notes that:

"It helps to have a virtually recession-proof economy, be well endowed with natural resources, and limiting foreign banks to a minor share of the market."

Perhaps the most balanced appraisal comes from US banker Bob Kelly, CEO of BNY Mellon, who headed up a Canadian bank before moving to the US:

"Canada is better managed than 20 years ago: they balanced the books, pre-funded social security, dealt with inflation and brought income tax rates down. In other words, better government! They have OSFI, a single regulator, which is more effective and efficient than the US patchwork. It's not just better regulation, but also the banking system reflects the economy in general."

France: the Commission Bancaire of the Banque de France

Profile

THE COMMISSION BANCAIRE, which has responsibility for banking supervision, is one of the three regulatory arms of the French central bank established by the Banking Act of 1984. It functions in parallel with the Banking and Financial Regulations Committee, which lays down the banking regulations, and the Credit Institutions and Investment Firms Committee, which grants authorisations.

The supervisory function is thus fully integrated into the central bank in terms of recruitment, training and other functions. The Commission Bancaire itself is made up of seven members and is chaired by the Governor of the Banque de France. Its brief is to protect depositors as well as act as a watchdog over the banking system to ensure its profitability and financial stability. It collaborates closely with the insurance regulator.

One of the distinguishing features of French banking supervision is its commitment to the active use of Pillar 2 measures to reflect macro-economic conditions as well as the risks undertaken by individual banks. A 10-page document on the Commission's website outlines in some detail such measures as the validation of bank risk models, the role of on-site inspections, the measures at the Commission's disposal to issue injunctions to adjust provisioning, modify a bank's organisation, limit its activities, and perhaps most important, to require additional capital above the minimum statutory requirements.

It is these proactive measures which have played a major role in the relative success of French bank regulation during the recent crisis. Several of our interviewees noted with surprise that large, complex banking groups like BNP Paribas have traversed the crisis without the massive losses suffered by other global peers. The well-publicised dealing losses incurred by Société Générale are attributed to management's having waived the existing protective measures such as a mandatory annual holiday for dealers, while Natixis' losses were suffered despite what we understand were capital requirements above the minimum.

The former head of the Commission Bancaire interviewed for this book, Jean-Louis Fort, attributes its relative success to several key policies and structures:

> "By far the most important success factor is proximity to the central bank. In a crisis you can demonstrate in dialogue with other bodies that the central bank is in control with the necessary insights and capabilities. Next is the equilibrium between central control and on-the-spot inspections: you can't control from reports sent to a central body, but you have to go out to the banks to check the reality. Thirdly, supervisors must have a long-term perspective and respect the fundamentals, avoiding fashions and bankers' arguments. At the time of the crisis we were told by bankers 'don't bother us with these rules,' and 'we can always get funding from the market.'
>
> "And our ability to vary capital ratios above the minimum – to say 'for you, the ratio is 12% not 8%' – is very important. It's imposed on all banks for the Tier 1 ratio on a very proactive basis. Supervisors must have a macro view and be able to enforce it."

M. Fort has strong views on the value of supervisors embedded in the banks as opposed to the process of on site-inspections:

> "The presence of 'censeurs' – essentially supervisors embedded in the major banks – was a defeat and removed in the 1960s. If you are integrated in a bank, it leads to becoming a prisoner of the bank."

One can assume that the Commission Bancaire is a strong voice for the implementation of Pillar 2 in the current discussions in Brussels on future regulation. As M. Fort, who was personally active in the debate leading to the present Pillar 2 structure, points out:

> "We wanted to make sure our successors would support the case by case approach to risk in the implementing of Pillar 1."

Germany: BaFin (Federal Financial Supervisory Authority)

Profile

BAFIN, GERMANY'S FINANCIAL SERVICES SUPERVISOR, was created in 2002 to combine the three previous regulators for banking, insurance and securities so as to establish a uniform national supervisor for all German financial institutions. Its mission is the stability and competitiveness of the German financial market.

BaFin supervises roughly 2,700 banks in addition to insurance companies and securities firms. It collaborates with the Bundesbank (the central bank) in its supervisory mission. To minimise duplication and make use of the Bundesbank's expertise and deep insights into the financial sector, the Bundesbank is assigned most of the operational tasks in banking supervision. It evaluates the audit and other reports submitted by the banks, carries on both routine and *ad hoc* prudential discussions with the banks. The Bundesbank carries out prudential audits of the banks and issues general rules and regulations.

The statutory role of BaFin is to close down or take other necessary action to solve problems in the sector, as well as issue general instructions laying down rules for carrying on banking business.

In practice, BaFin is the ultimate authority to enforce action in the banking sector. It also discusses the results of the Bundesbank's audit and field work and is responsible for writing a summary letter to the audited bank based on this analysis. In organisational terms, BaFin reports to the finance ministry, while the Bundesbank is independent of the ministry.

A major supervisory issue in Germany is the political influence of the German savings banks which are major stockholders in the regional *Landesbanken*. Initially designed to provide wholesale and other banking services to the locally-owned savings banks, during the past few decades the *Landesbanken* have expanded abroad and into areas such as commercial real estate which have generated substantial losses. In most cases the savings banks have recapitalised their respective *Landesbanken*, but efforts by BaFin to take preventive action have been forestalled in the national parliament by the influence of the savings banks.

The 2009 Federal election in Germany brought in a new government which has indicated its intention to merge BaFin into the Bundesbank.

Regarding the issue of governance with respect to the savings bank sector, Jochen Sanio points out that:

> "The responsibility for designing sound and effective governance mechanisms rests squarely with the public owners. Savings banks should be insulated as far as possible from political meddling and manoeuvring. If the public owners showed themselves incapable of fulfilling their obligations, regulators would have to step in with detailed prescriptions as to how business should be conducted in order to restrict imprudent behaviour."

Other perspectives

THE EXCERPT IN CHAPTER 6 from our interview with a major German bank confirms that BaFin's dilemma is well understood in its home market.

The same understanding does not seem widespread outside Germany, where a number of our interviewees attribute the multiple failures of *Landesbanken* to its regulator. One interviewee wonders whether "the regulator had his head in the sand". There is no particular reason why there should be total communication on the reality of regulatory performance around the world, but this apparent lack of understanding must add to the frustrations of BaFin's leadership.

Italy: Banca d'Italia

Profile

THE CURRENT ITALIAN BANK REGULATORY STRUCTURE – as well as that of the sector itself – is the product of an extended transformation of Italian banking from the Depression era, state-owned profile into the current privatised one which was codified by legislation in the 1990s. Since then, bank regulation and supervision has rapidly adopted the integrated model established by peer EU nations such as France and Spain. A critical factor in this politically-charged transition was the move of central bank head Carlo Azeglio Ciampi to the country's premiership.

The central bank, Banca d'Italia, has full responsibility for the regulation and supervision of financial institutions, while consumer and investor protection is the province of the securities regulator CONSOB. Within the central bank, the supervisory function is a separate department under a Director General, which functions in parallel with regulatory and other activities.

Our interview with the central bank pointed up the central importance of on-site visits in their supervisory process as well as the adoption several years ago of Pillar 2 supervision. Stress-testing of the major banks has been employed for several years. The result has been a relatively trouble-free passage of the Italian banks through the recent global crisis.

As our interviewee noted:

> "The most importance aspect of bank regulation is the ability to conduct effective on-site supervision. Banks are visited frequently for intensive due diligence. It requires quality people with an independent frame of mind and the ability to interact with both the banks and their colleagues as well as prepare informative reports. We have the impression

> that other regulators may not pay enough attention to this dimension."

Pillar 2 has been a major supervisory element for the past four to five years and has involved an active debate with the major banks. Management feels that the integration of regulation and supervision within the central bank is a major success factor. As our interviewee indicated:

> "There's great debate in Europe over whether to combine monetary policy and supervision. The Bank of Italy combines both. Supervisors find it useful to make use of monetary policy guidelines and insights and vice versa for the macro professionals – especially for systemic risk!"

A recent presentation on supervision by Giovanni Carosio, the Director General of the supervisory function, notes that:

> "Stress tests are by now an ordinary supervisory tool; the Bank of Italy, with the active participation of the banks, has promoted the corrective actions needed to refine and reinforce them ... In 2009, we intervened repeatedly to remind banks of the need for full compliance with the rules on corporate organisation and governance ... we asked the six largest banking groups to verify that their compensation and incentive schemes are also consistent with the Financial Stability Board's standards."

The availability of qualified professional staff is seen as a critical dimension in the supervisory role, and there is some concern in the Bank over the availability of this scarce resource in the future. As our interviewee pointed out:

> "Supervisors are not standard bureaucrats. If you're concerned about quality, you have to pay more. There's no question that remuneration levels between the supervisors and the best banks are very different, and it's worse elsewhere. It could be a problem in the next 10–15 years. The issue is how

to keep up-to-date on developments in banking. It's a sensitive issue which is not openly discussed."

At the top echelon, however, Bank of Italy executives have played a significant role on the European scene. Not only is the head of European bank supervision, Mario Draghi, also the Governor of the Italian central bank, but also the head of the EU supervisory body (CEBS) is Giovanni Carosio, the chief of the central bank's supervisory function. Several of our other interviewees have pointed to the importance of public confidence in such executives, especially in time of crisis as in the past few years, when politically sensitive decisions must be made.

Norway: Financial Supervisory Authority of Norway (Finanstylsynet)

Profile

NORWAY'S FINANCIAL SUPERVISORY AUTHORITY was created in 1994 following the country's financial crisis in which the major banks failed, were nationalised, and then successfully floated off to private investors. Since then, it has worked in harness with the country's other regulatory agencies – the finance ministry and Norges Bank (the central bank) – in a tripartite arrangement in which it provides the supervisory input eventually employed in finance ministry and other directives.

The Authority, which has responsibility for banking institutions and markets, is unusual globally in having employed from its formation in 1994 a macro-prudential strategy designed to contain systemic risks. It combines macro-analysis with its day-to-day supervisory insights; in effect, the macro views feed into the micro-supervision. Its approach involves analysis of systemic trends, interviews and on-site work with individual banks, internal discussion including the other members of the tripartite structure, advisory warnings to the banks as necessary, and, as appropriate, specific directives or guidance to the sector, as well as individual institutions.

In practice, this macro/micro approach has taken place in two sectors: commercial real estate and leveraged investment products sold to individual investors. For example, as real estate prices in Norway soared in 2006–07, the Authority analysed 11 Norwegian banks with heavy exposures in commercial real estate and notified them in 2008 of its concern over the adequacy of their capital base in the context of the ICAAP structure. No specific Tier 1 numbers were suggested, but as a result of this dialogue and market forces encouraging banks to build their capital base, Tier 1 ratios in Norway have risen on average from 6% to 10% since 2007.

In the investment sector, the Authority issued guidelines in 2004 on the use of leveraged loans to gear up on retail investment products, but the banks did not respond to these signals. A major investigation of over 300 products then indicated that such leverage actually reduced the likely return on the product below that of an ordinary bank deposit. The Authority then issued a final warning to banks in 2008 not to provide such leveraged finance.

When asked about the critical success factors behind the Authority's policy, a senior executive pointed to a number of key tenets:

> "One is close collaboration within the tripartite structure. It helps to be a small country; people went to school together. There's a close and open co-operation; all supervisory reports are made available to the central bank. We have no secrets!
>
> "Another is the experience of our people; most inspectors are career bankers with 10–15 years' experience; they know the industry.
>
> "And third is close contact with the top management of the banks. In the past few months I've met with the CEOs of the top seven banks in the country. The CEO must have knowledge of his bank's situation. But we leave the decisions to them; we don't give them a precise number for the ICAAP process but leave that to the bank and the market."

Other perspectives

NORWAY – OR, INDEED, SCANDINAVIA AS A WHOLE – is not on the radar of most of our interviewees, and Norway was selected as a case study to examine how a relatively small country with a successful banking system navigated the recent crisis. As in so many other cases, however, a multiplicity of factors may lie behind the perceived success or failure of the regulator. For example, in neighbouring Sweden, which also has its own challenges in exposure to the troubled Baltic region, a senior Swedish banker in referring to the Norwegian case study notes that:

> "Norway is a very domestic banking market. Honestly, Sweden could have looked like Norway if we didn't have a major international banking element."

Yet Norway's FSA has proved a useful example of many of the success factors present in markets which have attracted more public scrutiny. Being close to bank top management, recruiting experienced bankers, being proactive when issues are detected – all could be lessons for many other regulatory authorities.

Spain: Banca de España

Profile

THE BANCA DE ESPAÑA or Bank of Spain, the country's central bank as well as financial regulator, has exclusive responsibility for bank regulation in parallel with similar agencies covering insurance and securities. In our interviews, it was cited by a large number of our sources as one which had distinguished itself during the recent crisis as having been one of the few that took proactive steps before the crisis to address the issue of counter-cyclicality in lending, as well as taken a conservative view on capital allocation in the case of structured investment vehicle (SIV) off balance sheet vehicles.

As in other markets, its current regulatory powers were created in 1988 following massive banking losses for taxpayers and accounting manipulation at the end of the 1970s and early 1980s. Management at the time resisted the contemporary tide calling for the separation of supervision from central banking activities to ensure, among other things, that all the necessary information would be under the same roof.

Its regulatory brief covers the solvency and soundness of over 500 entities, of which some 360 are credit institutions, as well as a host of related objectives. Perhaps the unique organisational feature among its peers is the separation of bank supervision from bank regulation, each of which is managed by a Director General. The objective is to provide independent views from both regulatory and supervisory standpoints on banking issues as well as ensure a dialogue between the two. To quote a senior Bank of Spain executive:

> "It's the 'four eyes' concept: most other central banks combine the two into one structure. In our case, one sets the rules and the other enforces and executes them."

A senior Banco Santander executive, Vice-Chairman Matias Inciarte, highlighted this structure as a major differentiator in regulatory success:

> "The problem (driving the banking crisis) is not *regulation*, but the absence of *supervision*. The Bank of Spain told banks to consolidate SIVs, for example and other regulators didn't. Before the crisis, we were all wondering where there could be problems. The answer is that it's easy for the regulator to talk to the major banks and ask them if they see something of concern. That's what the Bank of Spain has done; they have more than 50 supervisors in our bank at any one time looking at what we're doing."

There has been an increase in recent years in on-site inspection as well as the permanent presence of 'embedded' inspection staff – as indicated in the Inciarte interview – in the major banks to provide insight. Its approach is generally characterised as 'very intense and close continuous monitoring'. Bank of Spain has also initiated a 'college of supervisors' structure for its two major banks, Santander and BBVA, with a number of peer regulators around the world.

Its proactive approach to bank regulation has featured two initiatives which have received widespread attention.

First, since 2000, the Bank has required banks to establish so-called dynamic provisions, or non-tax deductible general loss reserves in line with loan growth, rather than the traditional metric of level of non-performing or problem loans. This has not been well received by many banks, but the Bank of Spain has insisted on such a counter-cyclical approach. Our conversations with several Spanish banks indicate that the ability to release some of these reserves under current market conditions has had a positive impact on investors. The result has been to dampen considerably the impact in recent years of massive potential losses on mortgage loans.

Second, when the IFRS accounting standards were introduced in 2004, in order to be consistent with the new directive, the Bank of Spain took the conservative view that capital should be allocated to SIVs, or conduits, under *de facto* control of the banks, even though no ownership or guarantee linkage existed. Spanish banks complained that their global peers obtained more liberal regulatory treatment. The Spanish regulator held its ground, despite a debate with the accounting profession, and the SIV, or conduit, structure was not a feature of the Spanish financial scene.

While their regulatory reputation during the crisis has thus been enhanced, on the other hand market sources have been critical of the Bank of Spain for the massive build-up of mortgage loans and commercial real estate exposure in the country – despite the counter-cyclical build-up of loss reserves. A senior Bank of Spain supervisory executive interviewed for this book suggested that:

> "This case study should be written only after the outcome of this second crisis – a traditional banking cycle – in domestic real estate! The banks knew CME [commercial real estate] was very risky, but they still kept lending. The Bank of Spain couldn't evaluate the risk, and we trusted the banks. No one expected the depth of this recession."

Looking to the future, the Bank of Spain plans to continue its counter-cyclical regulation, while monitoring key trends such as rapid credit growth. On the key issue of innovation, it will monitor new product development carefully without stifling innovation – or, on the other hand, letting it explode.

Other perspectives

OUR OTHER INTERVIEWEES LAUDED the Bank of Spain's proactive initiatives described above, but generally pointed out that the bank must bear some responsibility for Spain's massive commercial real estate exposure.

Perhaps a more balanced account is given by the CEO of one of the major Spanish banks:

> "The Bank of Spain is on top of things. There's a closer involvement in the nitty gritty; they are more demanding than before. With separate securities and insurance jurisdictions, there's possibly an issue for the future, as they don't necessarily collaborate. The quality of supervisors has improved dramatically; they can understand and deal with an actual situation, rather than just apply rules. With regard to the overall level of bank problem loans, this is a political issue. The Bank of Spain has argued for independence like the US Fed, but they don't have the political clout, as regional governments have their own powers over the local *cajas*."

The ultimate accolade for the Bank of Spain comes from a respected peer. The former Supervisor Jean-Louis Fort at the Commission Bancaire points out with reference to dynamic provisioning:

> "The Spanish had the guts to do it; our authorities turned down our recommendation to do it!"

UK: Financial Services Authority (FSA)

Profile

FORMED IN 2000 when the regulatory authority over UK financial institutions was split off from the central bank, the Bank of England, the FSA regulates all providers of financial services in the UK. It is accountable to the UK Treasury and is funded by the firms it supervises.

The FSA has three strategic aims:

- To promote efficient, orderly and fair markets;
- To help retail consumers achieve a fair deal; and
- To improve its business capability and effectiveness.

From the outset, the FSA has maintained a principles-based rather than a rules-based approach. Its response to risks identified in the financial system is proportionate to the risks involved. Thus its ARROW risk-based supervision evaluates the relative threat to its statutory objectives. ARROW stands for Advanced Risk Response Operating framework. Firms are assigned to one of four supervision categories, based on the risk they pose to the FSA's objectives, as perceived by the FSA. The ARROW framework describes how the FSA assesses the risk. Although the requirements are the same for all firms, the level of the FSA's involvement depends on the supervision category. Firms in category A can expect a close and continuous relationship; those in category D can expect little or no individual contact.

With regulatory responsibility for some 29,000 financial providers, overwhelmingly small firms such as insurance brokers and financial advisors, the FSA inevitably devotes most of its resources to such small firms. The bulk of its total staff of roughly

2,900 thus deal with customer protection issues, and a major strategic retail initiative is named 'Treating Customers Fairly'.

At the same time, it regulates some of the largest, most sophisticated and complex financial institutions in what is one of the world's leading financial centres. For such firms, the ARROW risk-based evaluation process is at the core of its supervisory efforts.

A key event in the FSA's history was the collapse of Northern Rock in the summer of 2007, which coincided with the onset of the recent financial crisis in other markets such as the US. The ARROW process had not anticipated the collapse of the wholesale markets on which Northern Rock's funding strategy was based, and the photos in the press of queues of depositors lined up for days in front of Northern Rock's branches had a major impact on the public mind as well as focus on bank regulation. Since then the FSA has made a major effort to introduce stress testing of capital and liquidity as well as other measures.

A senior FSA executive interviewed for this book summarises the transformation which the agency has undergone since the events of 2007:

> "The FSA made mistakes (e.g. in the case of Northern Rock) but owned up to them and is now more proactive on issues such as capital. As banks in the US and UK failed, the FSA took a hard look at how much capital might be needed in stress situations. We now take a forward look at the institution: how it will survive under stress, and the need for major increases in capital and liquidity."

This more intense level of supervision is a demanding one in terms of the availability of the skills needed to regulate effectively the large, complex global banks under its responsibility. Subsequent chapters deal in more detail with these challenges as well as provide some off- the-record views of several interviewees whose firms are regulated by the agency.

Other perspectives

THE FSA'S OVERALL FUTURE ROLE is open to debate, as there is a school of thought that its regulatory function should be passed to the Bank of England, leaving the FSA with only a consumer protection role. However, even if there is no change in its functions, it faces considerable challenges.

A former FSA executive articulates the challenge for the future for the FSA:

> "Its challenge is how to allocate a limited number of highly skilled professionals to a large number of potential problem institutions. Would Northern Rock have been perceived to be a systemic risk in 2006? No! It's a case of appalling regulation, but no surprise! The FSA is doing well on pay, and they've done it by spending lots of money. There may be push-back in the future on the issue of money. And it has been done by taking risk; there must be lots of firms which are getting less attention but are not on the high-risk list."

Another regulator notes the multiplicity of the FSA's tasks:

> 'The FSA suffers from having about five missions and eight formal statutory constraints: a ridiculously complicated task for any organisation'.

A veteran London-based banker also cites possible overstretch:

> "The FSA talks about being principles-based, but I never understood what it means! The FSA was hooked on it, but the rule book runs to hundreds of pages. It's neither principles nor rules-based; they picked and chose what they wanted. There were broad principles, like controls, but they had all the tools to do what they wanted. They are overstretched in mandates – including financial advertising, promoting the London market, and mortgages. There's great

reliance on banks' senior management and the quantity of MIS. There's a small staff, low budget, but enormous remit. But can anyone have achieved these goals?"

The Chairman of a major UK bank also notes the challenge of overstretch:

> "The FSA's TCF (Treating Customers Fairly) agenda seemed to be the primary preoccupation in its dialogue with us."

A final comment comes from another former FSA executive:

> "The most difficult challenge will be: can you really spot the risk and address it? You need effective communication with the central bank but you can make it work in a variety of ways – not just by merger with them! In Northern Rock, they got the wrong risk, but the system is only as good as the people using it to spot really important risks."

US: The Federal Reserve, Office of Comptroller of the Currency, SEC, and FDIC

Profile

BANKS IN THE US can be chartered and supervised by regulators at either the national or state level, while today's key regulatory agencies are products of historical financial crises: the Panic of 1907 and the Great Depression of the 1930s. The recent banking crisis in turn has generated heated discussion over the county's future regulatory structure which at the time of writing had not been resolved.

The country's Founding Fathers in the 1790s disagreed sharply on the value of a central banking institution, and only in 1913, following the Panic of 1907, was the Federal Reserve System created. As a balance between central authority and decentralised regional units owned by member banks, the Fed is only one of four bank regulatory agencies at the federal level, with overall responsibility, among other things, for the safety and soundness of the banking system as well as specific regulatory responsibility for bank holding companies and the US operations of foreign banks.

Three other agencies at federal level also have regulatory responsibilities. The Office of Comptroller of the Currency, a branch of the US Treasury, supervises nationally chartered banks. The Federal Deposit and Insurance Corporation (FDIC), created in the Depression year of 1933, has a dual role of providing deposit insurance as well as supervision of state chartered banks which not members of the Federal Reserve System. Finally, the Office of Thrift Supervision regulates thrifts, or savings banks, which include, among other institutions, the thrift affiliate of AIG, the troubled global insurer.

In addition, the Securities and Exchange Commission (SEC), which had regulatory authority over the Wall Street investment banks, relinquished this authority during the recent crisis in favour of the Federal Reserve.

At state level, banks can be chartered and regulated by authorities in one of the country's 50 states. All state chartered banks are regulated by their state; in addition, they are supervised by the Fed if members of the Federal Reserve System, or, if not, by the FDIC. Thus a number of US banks are co-regulated by both state and national agencies.

Finally, the decentralised character of the US banking system is reinforced by the presence of 12 regional banks comprising the Fed system. Each of these is owned by member banks, with local bankers represented on their regional boards, which in turn make up a portion of the Fed Board in Washington. In practice, major Fed decisions on a troubled bank may need to take into consideration the view of regional interests.

The recent banking crisis tested the US regulatory system both at the individual supervisory level and in the decision-making process among agencies. In practice, the OTS did not play a significant role in the bailout of AIG, despite its nominal regulatory role. In the discussions over funding several bailout deals, the FDIC was involved because of the difficulty of locating sufficient available funding and the presence of its massive reserves.

Thus most mid-sized and large US banks are regulated by at least one agency, and each such agency has its own agenda. While the concept of a 'council of regulators' has been discussed, there appears to be little collaboration among such co-regulators. As indicated in Chapter 6, political factors drive these agendas.

Other perspectives

FOR OUR INSIGHTS on US regulation, we relied essentially on individuals outside the regulatory world – in large part because of the sensitivity of the current debate. Many of these insights have been recorded in earlier chapters, but here we select a few from sources who have an interesting overall perspective on the issues.

One of the US federal supervisors interviewed summarises his perspective off the record:

> "In the US, there are lots of fires going on in different agencies – different points of view. In hindsight, we looked at individual banks. It's OK to take assets off the balance sheet, but we never sat back and asked 'what if everyone did it?' There won't be a global regulator; we can't even do it in the US! There are too many constituencies. There's better sharing of data, but is that 'information'?"

A senior US banker, referring to the widespread US practice of embedding supervisors in banks such as his, concludes:

> "In the US, intrusiveness hasn't worked. It's an unbelievable patchwork!"

A retired CEO of a US regional bank which has three regulators notes:

> "We had 60–100 regulators in the bank full-time; there was lots of supervision! The US is NOT the model for the future. It's handicapped by the competing priorities of the regulators and the political dynamic of the day – like compliance, the CRA (Community Reinvestment Act), etc. Everything is supervised!"

An Australian regulator concludes:

> "The chaotic shambles in the US is a – fortunately unique – example of many regulators trying to do the same thing – often to the same entities. Let's hope the US fixes that."

Lessons from the case studies

THIS SELECTION OF NINE NATIONAL CASE STUDIES of regulatory performance cannot be regarded as a league table of success or failure. A number of other successful regulators were suggested by a few of our sources, but we have been unable to include them in this volume.

For example, the key regulatory role of the central bank in Brazil's remarkable economic performance may deserve a chapter on its own. Pedro Moreira Salles, Chairman of the country's largest private sector bank, Itaú Unibanco, offers a summary of best regulatory practice stemming in large part from successful emergence from a banking crisis:

> "Because we went through a banking crisis in the 1990s, with the end of inflation, the central bank improved its oversight and regulatory framework 15 years ago. You don't have off balance sheet vehicles. Everything has to be consolidated. The balance sheets are not leveraged. The exposure to mortgages is very low – perhaps 2% of GDP."

But by drilling down into the track record of our sample of nine, with the help of other informed observers, one can at least identify what works and what doesn't in the bank supervisory business. Here are some suggested conclusions from their experience.

Lessons from experience

- **The US stands out as the problem child in the regulatory universe.** Not only does the US financial market dominate the globe in terms of size and sophistication – as the sub-prime toxin proved in the recent crisis – but also the most problematic in the critical dimension of political conflict. Our sources could provide no light at the end of this tunnel. Politics may bedevil regulation in markets like Germany and Spain, but in the US it dominates the scene.

- **Multiple bank regulators – not only in the US – can hamper overall effectiveness as well as increase costs.** In Germany, BaFin reached a satisfactory arrangement with the Bundesbank to share the regulatory and supervisory responsibilities, but it appears that different mandates, possible gaps and personal agendas can often get in the way of effective supervision.
- **If supervision is separate from the central bank, excellent communication between the two agencies is a critical success factor.** A number of highly successful supervisory agencies such as those in Canada and Australia have been spun out of the central bank, but apparently succeed only with such close collaboration. In contrast, the UK's FSA had the same origins but apparently without the close working relationship – unless it is restored by any potential change in ruling political party or government policy.
- **It is extraordinarily difficult – at least to the outsider – to determine the respective contribution of the regulator/supervisor and other variables, such as economic conditions, banking structures and risk appetite.** To complicate the judgement, even the best regulators, such as some of those in this chapter, do not have an impeccable track record of success. But at least this chapter has identified the qualities which mark the successful regulator. And good luck – such as economic conditions – can be one of these qualities.
- **A proactive stance – supported by the ability to identify systemic risks – is a major success factor.** Taking on the top management of a major bank, in particular

when the action could take the punchbowl away from the party, requires strong backbone. A corollary of this stance is the ability, as in the case of the Canadian and Australian authorities, to target individual institutions in their dictates. One size does not necessarily fit all banking institutions in a given market. Arguably the UK's FSA has historically taken too permissive or collaborative a stance, but it is difficult to see how the agency could have identified Northern Rock as a systemic risk.

- **In most national markets, the central bank tends to be the repository of superior talent as well as public confidence.** Brains and brand combined are a powerful magnet. It is thus a natural home for the supervisory function, assuming those qualities can be extended to that function. The challenge for an independent supervisor is thus to carve out its own identity while maintaining a collaborative stance, sharing information, and taking effective action.
- **Successful supervisors must focus on their key role: to identify risks and take the necessary action to mitigate them.** The UK FSA appears to be a case study of too broad a remit given the challenges of a large and dynamic financial sector. By the same token, the gaps and overlaps in the US regulatory structure diminish their ability to fulfil this central role.

But experience shows how difficult it is to identify systemic risks. Håkan Berg, a senior Swedbank executive with current responsibility for their Baltic businesses, notes that 20/20 hindsight is present in criticism of the Swedish banks and regulators for not having taken action to forestall the banks' heavy investment in the troubled Baltic region:

> "With hindsight it's easy to see the problems! The reality is that the Baltic problems were identified too late. We all

made mistakes, but there was no pressure from the regulators in 2007/8 to slow the Baltic expansion. We all agreed there would be a Baltic downturn, but also agreed there would be a soft landing. But with the global recession, which wasn't predicted, a lot of things combined so there was no soft landing!"

- **The 'old-fashioned' way to regulate described seems to work the best, in the view of many of our sources.** One can argue the virtues of principles or rules-based regulation, but the 'old-fashioned' tools of a LTV or leverage ratio, increasing the capital base, and banning toxic products seem to add the most value for the successful regulators described above. (See Chapter 8.)
- **Strong views – pro and con – are expressed on the issue of embedded supervisors vs. periodic on-site visits.** In Europe alone, we found Banca de España comfortable with the former, while its peers in France and Italy are committed to in-depth on-site visits instead. Elsewhere, we found trenchant criticism of embedded supervisors in the US, while the FSA in the UK is increasing the number of supervisors assigned to specific banks. The Banca d'Italia's Roberto Violi summarises a view on embedding:

"Embedding is not wrong per se, but you need an arm's length relationship with the bank – be close but not too close!"

- **Implementation of proactive Pillar 2 initiatives also divides the agencies profiled.** At one extreme, the French, Spanish, Italian and Norwegian, as well as the Canadian and Australian, supervisors have followed some or all of the recommendations of the existing Pillar 2 guidelines. One can only imagine the debate between them and their

Anglo-Saxon peers as the current efforts to establish global guidelines progress.

In conclusion, one returns to the list of critical success factors listed above by Robert Albertson. It is a monumental task – especially the last factor of avoiding unintended consequences, which is the challenge today as regulators devise new rules on a global scale – a topic we discuss in the next chapter.

Chapter 8: Lessons from the past and the outlook for the future

"We will have grown up when we stop blaming regulators for a failure of a bank." (Mervyn King, Governor of the Bank of England (quoted in the *Financial Times*, 27 January 2010)

Searching finance

THIS CHAPTER SUMMARISES THE VIEWS of our interviewees on several fundamental questions. What can we learn from the experience of regulation during the crisis? In effect, what works and what does not? Is regulation likely to prevent future banking crises? What will be the likely success of the current macro-prudential efforts being made in Brussels, Basel and the US to implement the new regulatory framework at the global, European and national levels?

Our own views on these questions will be found in the final and concluding Chapter 9.

Our interview findings can perhaps best be structured around the following questions asked during the interview process:

- What is the purpose of bank prudential regulation?
- What works in bank regulation?
- What does NOT work in regulation?
- How effective will the current macro-prudential approach be in the future?
- And finally, the big question: can we avoid the next banking crisis?

What is the purpose of bank prudential regulation?

FOR MOST OF OUR INTERVIEWEES, this is the fundamental question with which to begin the debate. For some, it is the absence of bank failures. Several current and past UK regulators have well-thought out views.

For an executive of the FSA:

> "The appropriate analogy is the classic dilemma of the policeman and the traffic lights. It's a tough test. If there are lots of accidents at the lights, the policeman apparently failed. But to judge him, you would need to know a lot more about

the situation: was there a lot of traffic, what was the weather, were there lots of drunken drivers at the time, etc. For example, look at BaFin in Germany; lots of bank failures with no regulatory action, but you have to ask the question, why? What is the standard for bank supervision? If the failure of a unit is the failure of the supervisor, we'll need LOTS more capital. If it's zero failures, we'll need much higher liquidity and capital, which means higher bank margins, leading to more intermediation to other markets."

Former FSA executive Michael Foot raises the issue of stifling innovation through over-regulation:

> "For example, Direct Line in the UK motor insurance sector as a newcomer cut prices and offered better service. Traditional insurers said it would be a catastrophe and would destroy the industry. But customers got cheap insurance and prices dropped. The danger is that regulators will stop this from happening."

Another former FSA executive, Clive Briault, believes that:

> "The question for the future is whether good regulation is just more and more regulation, or whether it actually identifies and addresses the most important risks. And what happens if no-one sees the next crisis coming – just as no-one believed that liquidity in the wholesale markets could dry up as spectacularly as it did in 2007 and 2008, with severe consequences for both commercial and investment banks? Banks take risks and bank failures cannot be eliminated entirely."

Another issue is raised by Sir Win Bischoff, a veteran UK investment banker and now Chairman of Lloyds Banking Group:

> "The major culprit (behind the recent financial crisis) is bank management; you can't blame the clients or the regulators. And don't blame the politicians! The buck stops with

bank management. Most of the information regulators get is from bankers. Unless banks see the danger, it's unlikely that the regulators would pick it up. Regulators aren't smarter than bankers. And if bankers didn't see it, it's not surprising that regulators didn't."

What works in bank regulation?

OUR SOURCES AGREE on two key success factors. The first is the **primacy of risk assessment** as the regulator's role. The case studies in Chapter 7 of APRA, OSFI and other successful regulators confirms that evaluating the capacity of individual banks to mitigate risk, for example in a housing bubble, is central to their role. Then, having determined that this risk needs to be mitigated, the second success factor is to **take action**, usually in the form of applying targeted penalties such as a higher capital ratios, lower LTV components, or higher loan down-payments for the system or individual banks. And one size does not fit all; the most highly regarded regulators do not hesitate to tailor their intervention to the circumstances of individual banks.

Former FSA regulator Clive Briault summarises the progress of many regulators in this process:

> "There are three steps: identify risks, decide what to do about them, and then do it! This time (for the recent crisis) we got one and half steps there! A considerable amount of analysis of risks to financial stability was being undertaken before 2007. Internationally, the IMF profiled the growth of balance of payment imbalances. But neither the US nor China took action on these imbalances. In the UK the risks of a reversal in house prices was well analysed and documented before 2007 in the Bank of England's Financial Stability Report and the Financial Services Authority's

> Financial Risk Outlook. But the focus was on credit risk: did individual banks have enough capital to survive a major drop in house prices?
>
> "The FSA did an analysis of the potential impact on banks of a 20% fall in house prices and this was reflected in individual capital requirements for individual banks and in the assumptions that had to be included in their internal models for calculating capital requirements. But this protection against credit risk proved to be inadequate to protect many banks against the shocks to the availability of liquidity in 2007 and 2008."

Risk assessment is therefore central to bank regulation. Goldman Sachs is widely regarded as a leader in such assessment. Asked what his recommendations for best practice in future regulation would be, Managing Director Lucas Van Praag understandably focuses on such an assessment, which underpins Goldman's own risk management strategy:

> "Regulators must understand a bank's true exposure to risk. Fair valuing assets, or marking to market, allows banks to recognise their exposures quickly and value them appropriately. If you're a capital markets player, not marking to market is like taking off in a plane and flying blind into the clouds. Second, risk and control functions must be completely independent from the business units. If there is a question about a mark or a disagreement about a risk limit, the risk manager's view should always prevail."

Even the best risk management talent, however, can identify the wrong risk. A senior Citibank executive describes the efforts made as early as 2005 by a group called the Counterparty Risk Management Policy Group, which consisted of the top risk managers from the major global banks and reported to Gerry Corrigan of Goldman Sachs. Our interviewee reports that:

> "There was a high sense of comfort in 2005 on the issue of counterparty risk, in particular the completeness of documentation and risk for investors. But we missed the issue of complexity in the structured products being created with this counterparty risk. The game was lost in the summer of 2007. People danced around the issue! No one addressed complexity, and there was a breakdown in credit product standards to push product out the door."

There is thus a need for highly experienced human talent able not only to identify risks but also to deal effectively with senior bank management to enforce the regulator's conclusions. As Chapter 7 indicates, the success of regulators in countries like Norway, Canada and Australia can be attributed in large part to their recruitment of seasoned talent, often from the banks themselves, who understand banking and are focused on proactive supervision.

Is there a need for a new approach to bank regulation? Many say there is not. As one senior US banker says:

> "Regulators with good track records in the crisis – many of them in emerging markets – stuck with traditional approaches. They didn't rely on principles-based or model-driven supervision but instead enforced loan to deposit and leverage ratios, and placed restrictions on structured products and sub-prime. And yet they were criticised for being 'old fashioned'."

BCG's Andy Maguire agrees:

> "What rules to use for the future? I believe in simple rules that have worked – like the leverage ratios that were thrown away in the past. In other words, a small number of rules that have made sense in the past – not a multitude of detailed rules or forced compliance. Rather than collect the rule book, it's more like a few principles and good tests; and constantly challenge the banks."

Eric Gerding in a special issue of *Lombard Street* also believes in rules that pass the 'granny' test:

> "We don't need to invent new regulatory tools: inspection, disclosure and capital/leverage requirements will do just fine."

Another lesson from the successful agencies is excellent communications between the bank CEO and his counterpart in the regulatory agency. HSBC Chairman Stephen Green agrees that:

> "We need communication with both the technical regulatory team and the high level relationship – a 1:1 interface between the head of the agency and the CEO or Chairman – perhaps four meetings a year. In effect, a 'close and continuous' relationship!"

Some regulators and observers distinguish between a principles-based and a rules-based approach. For most of our sources, this is a semantic issue. Either or both can be relevant in a particular situation. Principles are a necessary framework for the regulator, but the principle of risk mitigation should be the dominant one. Rules are necessary for supervision, but not an oversized rule book that should not be dropped on one's foot! And the fewer rules the better, if only to minimise the inevitable efforts by banks to subvert them – the classic problem of unexpected consequences.

David Llewellyn of Loughborough University sums up his profile of the ideal bank regulator:

> "An institutional structure that makes it absolutely clear who is responsible for what; not relying on regulation alone but taking early corrective action; being prepared to intervene early and being very brave, saying 'we don't like what you're doing', and recognising that when things seem to be going well is exactly the time when things start to go wrong!"

What does NOT work in regulation?

MANY OF OUR SOURCES ARE HIGHLY CRITICAL of the dispersal of supervisory talent, especially that embedded in the banks being supervised and focusing essentially on compliance and audit-type tasks, as well as the possibility of so-called regulatory capture. Chapter 6 discusses this issue in some detail.

A senior risk manager in a German bank summarises the views of many of our sources:

> "How can you supervise banks if you don't understand the business and the products?"

So-called 'light touch' regulation has not proven particularly effective. The UK FSA, for example, began life in a boom period with this approach, which assumed that market discipline would be effective.

Finally, gaps in regulatory authority – or agencies ill-equipped to deal with the risks being undertaken by banks – certainly are a major source of concern. As discussed above, the US regulatory scene – currently being debated in Washington – is of fundamental importance to global regulation.

How effective will the current macro-prudential approach be in the future?

AS INDICATED ABOVE, efforts to improve bank regulation and supervision are now focused on the systemic impact of market and other forces on the banking system and individual institutions. Often termed macro-prudential regulation, as a parallel to the macro-economic powers exercised by central banks in managing interest rates and the money supply, it is the current preoccupation of the authorities in Basel and Brussels, as well as the US and other markets.

Our interviewees were asked how effective they believed these efforts would be in improving the effectiveness of bank regulation.

The responses were largely equivocal. In sum, macro is a good idea, but with an uncertain outcome.

Many of our sources pointed out that macro regulation is not a new concept. Pillar 2 of the current Basel II framework, which focuses on the role of the supervisor, has been in place for decades. Yet many European authorities, as well as the US, have failed to incorporate it in their actual practice. Key elements of the text of Pillar 2 are provided in Appendix 1 to provide a benchmark for the current discussions over macro-prudential guidance. In brief, it is based on four principles:

1 The bank's processes for adjusting capital based on its overall risk profile, or the ICAAP;
2 Supervisory review of this capital assessment;
3 The expectation by the supervisor that the bank will hold more capital than the statutory minimum if necessary; and
4 The obligation of the supervisor to intervene to prevent capital from falling below the amount necessary to support the risks.

Management consultant Dominik Treeck of Oliver Wyman provides a thoughtful forecast:

> "A new model – overlaying macro- on micro-prudential supervision – makes good sense and is promising, but all depends on the execution! It would constitute great progress if we could create a macro-prudential policy maker with the same level of independence as some central banks have in regard to monetary policy, with a clear mandate and ac-

countability. How should the system be recast? Who should play that role? The central bank has powerful, independent tools to manage monetary policy, but the same is not true for macro-prudential policy. Execution depends on implementation on the micro-prudential level. What does that mean? Should the central bank manage micro supervision, or can we keep it separate?"

The Norwegian regulator Bjørn Skogstad Aamo notes that:

"Since 1994 we've had a macro system as part of our regulatory work. We saw the limitations of a lack of macro in the crisis on the 1990s and now have people with a macro background in place. With the strong growth of commercial real estate exposure in 2006/7, we organised a series of theme inspections in the banks most exposed and asked for more prudence in financing real estate developments. The exposure in this area was then included in the general ICAAP process (Pillar 2 of the Basel II system) in 2008–09 in which we applied pressure which raised the Norwegian banks' Tier 1 ratio from 6% to about 10%. So we had in place a kind of macro framework. We travelled in 1994–05 to see other regulators in Europe but found their approach very rudimentary!"

Thus implementation of the concept of Pillar 2 has been uneven. In Asia-Pacific, for example, a senior Fitch executive notes that most countries disregarded it, but in Hong Kong, with the legacy of the old Bank of England, the HKMA (Hong Kong Monetary Authority) has imposed higher capital requirements. In the same region, however, APRA has espoused its principles.

Thus a senior regulator points out that:

"Actually, Pillar 2 is simply good micro supervision of systemically important institutions, particularly in regimes such as Australia in which the supervisor can set individual bank capital ratios and issue statutory directions. We have been operating on a *de facto* Pillar 2 approach for as long as anybody can remember, which goes back to the 1990s."

Former FSA regulator Clive Briault believes that implementing a macro approach would be

> "... a hell of a job! It is important to undertake macro-prudential oversight, but it is also important to be realistic about the difficulties in spotting all of the right risks; in identifying what actions should be taken to address these risks; and in implementing these actions at times when they may be politically unpopular. 'Ending the party' may be attractive to a risk-averse regulator or central banker, but it may look less attractive to a politician facing re-election in six months' time. And risk aversion can be taken too far – a completely safe financial system would not serve a useful purpose in providing the financial intermediation that transforms short-term deposits into long-term lending. The system will be better, but there's still a risk of either doing too little or going too far and being too safe."

One of the national regulatory heads participating in the Committee of European Bank Supervisors quoted in Chapter 4 provides a fascinating glimpse into the current dialogue in Brussels:

> "The big question is how to organise the regulatory structure. We need macro supervision; no-one in Europe had it. Micro supervision didn't see the consequences of geographic diversification and entering riskier markets. You need both macro and micro. There are two views: the specialist supervisors say they can incorporate macro in their micro supervision and are best equipped because they know the banks; the other view is to merge macro and micro supervision into the central bank."

At the centre of this dialogue is Jochen Sanio of BaFin, a member of the recently established global Financial Stability Board (FSB), who must also deal with the unique German dimension of a rule-of-law based national governance. In his view,

> "Macro-regulation is currently still under construction. We're trying to push this on both a European and a global level. But it will be very difficult to know precisely how future macro-economic developments will pan out. Regulators have to accept that they do not have a crystal ball and face the grim reality that there are limits to knowledge.
>
> "With the formation of the FSB, for the first time ever we have a new structure and process at the political level, in which finance ministries are involved in designing new rules to strengthen financial stability on a global level. If something is agreed in the FSB, the G20 (ministers and/or heads of governments) can be expected to endorse it. The chair of FSB is the only person in international regulation who has direct access to the G20 heads of governments, which shows what an important role the FSB will play in the process of international regulation from now on."

A similar view on the outlook for future global regulation comes from a senior UK banker:

> "The new banking authority for the EU is a force to be recognised – a new feature of supervision. It will not have an arbitrary power over national jurisdictions, but if it's staffed well and has teeth it can be the basis for its own dialogue with the banks. But the macro committee with a view on systemic risk at the EU level sounds like another unwieldy structure with all 27 members involved."

A thoughtful view of the outlook for macro-prudential regulation is provided by Ted Price at OSFI, one of the success stories in national regulation:

"What is the future of macro regulation? Concerns over systemic impact are important, but every 10–15 years there has been a banking crisis of some type, it will be something else next time – it's the nature of the beast. Regulators are good at avoiding the last crisis, but have to keep an eye on the future. Macro-prudential monitoring will help in indicating where we are in the cycle, but strong supervision of individual institutions is more important, as a strong financial system is made up of strong banks."

Two negative comments on macro regulation come from the US. Bank analyst Robert Albertson is pessimistic:

"What will come of it? Just about nothing! It would have helped if people had said 'we've got to act!' There's been a lack of will. You can centralise regulatory power, but would it have prevented what happened? There's nothing wrong with CDOs; even sub-prime is OK, but they can be fatally misused under flawed assumptions. In a way, we're blaming the gun for the murder! It was perfectly clear in 2005/6 in looking at the pretty graphs on US housing loan assumptions in investor presentations. There were no negative price projections. Look at their assumptions – all based on rising house prices; no-one thought they could be flat or fall, much less fall by 35%."

And former US bank CEO Larry Fish opines:

"I'm fairly pessimistic about anything happening. What supervision needs is to prioritise what they supervise – continue to oversee compliance and community development but re-emphasise risk and liquidity. In other words, more micro-supervision of off balance sheet risks, capital markets, liquidity and capital adequacy."

And finally the big question: can we avoid the next banking crisis?

WE NOW REVERT now back to the original question at the beginning of this chapter: what is the purpose of regulation? On the minds of most observers, the central question is simple: what are the chances of preventing future bank crises?

The response of our sources is clear: crises will continue to happen. From the top – Mario Draghi – down, we must prepare for more bank failures and financial crises.

In his November 2009 presentation to the Conference of ECB-CFS Research Network, *Challenges to Financial Stability and the Proposals of the Financial Stability Board,* Draghi is clear:

> "Can we prevent the next crisis? Almost by definition of the word 'crisis', the response to this question is bound to be negative. But what we can and should do is to make our financial system more resilient when the next crisis hits it."

For McKinsey management consultant Patrick Butler, the outlook is a sombre one:

> "We need proper regulation, tougher than that on the table today. If we are courageous enough to implement unpopular measures, and courageous enough to enable the supervisors to enforce it, it will reduce the risk of future crises. But it will not prevent them. There have been dozens of banking crises over the last 30 years, and there will be more and more on a Richter scale comparable to 2008. It is absolutely essential therefore that we get to grips with Too Big To Fail. We must develop both the approach and the will to allow large banks to fail. Without this, not only will there be more failures, but the human and social costs will again be enormous."

Investment banker Lucas van Praag of Goldman Sachs is more guarded:

"Preventing the next crisis is high on the agenda, but can anyone predict what the next one is? There is a lot of push for regulatory action, but the water is muddied by several issues, including a lack of consensus on the causes of the current crisis. It is important that in our efforts to prevent the next unforeseen crisis, we do not inadvertently hinder the innovation needed for economic growth."

A senior US banker is equally uncertain:

"How successful might the new regulatory structure be? No-one knows! The next issue will be something we haven't focused on: there is a danger we'll fight the last war. Policy makers have to decide what the banking system is supposed to do. Glass-Steagall introduced in the 1930s was eventually overtaken by events. The spirit of the times changed."

We turn now to the final chapter with our own views on the issues.

Chapter 9: Conclusions

Searching finance

THIS FINAL CHAPTER summarises our own conclusions from this research. It has been a unique experience to gather the off-the-record views of experienced regulators, bankers, academics, consultants, rating agencies and bank analysts. And to do it in the shadow of the daily headlines, announcing yet new initiatives in bank regulation, heightens the sense of participation! This story will clearly run and run as the regulatory environment continues to develop and change under the spotlight of current and future events; here we present our views as of the time of writing in early 2010.

Our observations fall under the broad topics as follows:

- The likelihood of future banking crises;
- What regulatory action can be taken to minimise their impact;
- Redefining 'regulation' and 'supervision';
- The quality and availability of regulatory and supervisory skills;
- The core issue of politics;
- The likelihood of a level playing field between bank regulators around the world;
- The danger of over-regulation; and
- The role of bank management.

The likelihood of future banking crises

THERE WILL BE MORE BANKING CRISES and bailouts in the future which cannot be identified today.

Mario Draghi's comment in Chapter 8 has been echoed by many of our interviewees. Acknowledging this is fundamental to future regulation. The role of regulation will be to minimise the number and impact of such banking failures, not to prevent them. Predicting the nature of future crises is bound to be an exercise in frustration – albeit a cornerstone of the regulatory challenge. And predicting where it will strike will be equally challenging. We do not recall ANY wise man who predicted publicly, for example, the global collapse of liquidity which sank Northern Rock in mid-2007. As so many of our sources pointed out, it is quite likely that the next crisis will probably be a totally new one and not on today's agenda.

In this context, today's focus on likely suspects such as Too Big to Fail (TBTF) and narrow vs. casino banking is beside the point. As bank strategy consultants, we have difficulty swallowing the suggestion of breaking up massive yet highly successful and well-managed banks such as HSBC and JPMorgan simply to satisfy the perceived need for a target for blame. Yes, management failures drove most of the bailouts, but they involved banks and other financial institutions of all shapes and sizes.

One good reason for clarifying this point is the famous argument of moral hazard well known to insurers and now to bankers. For any regulator to decree publicly in advance that any bank, whatever its profile, will be bailed out, could well encourage management to create the conditions to require that action. The experience of 2007–09 should teach us all that the relationship between banks and the public authorities is a close and dynamic one, with these authorities needing to make a judgement – however imperfect – in each case as to whether support is necessary for the public good. For anyone interested in this subject, Sorkin's excellent book 'Too Big to Fail' should be required reading.

The effect of regulatory action on future crises

WHAT CAN REGULATORS DO to minimise the number and impact of future bank crises and failures?

Both macro- and micro-prudential efforts must be improved to detect possible future problems.

The first step is to improve the regulator's ability to identify generic or bank-specific problems. The 'what if' stress testing of highly regarded regulators such as APRA, OSFI, Banque de France and the Norwegian authorities – admittedly applied to a standard price bubble such as house prices – should pay off if the appropriate human resources are devoted to the task. We discuss below the structural implications of this challenge. Other problems can be identified by such techniques as mark-to-market pricing, if a market exists. For example, Lucas van Praag, Managing Director at Goldman Sachs, as a firm one of the best risk managers in the business, pointed out to us that in early 2007 the firm had a long position in sub-prime assets. By noting a fall in sub-prime prices, management debated the situation and moved to a short position, thereby becoming one of the few institutions to earn money on that toxic product. A final approach might be to engage independent risk management experts on a contractual basis to supplement in-house skills. An analogy in the US could be the recruitment of a team of private equity specialists to break up General Motors in 2009, rather than rely on public servants to carry out this complex and difficult task.

The second step is to take action by challenging management and being prepared to enforce that challenge. Again, our group of successful regulators did so in Australia, Norway and Canada, applying simple metrics such as lower LTV and higher Tier 1 ratios. This did not happen to a sufficient extent in the US and

UK, whose banks suffered heavily from the crisis. We discuss below the skills and mandates of those who provide this challenge. And the current discussions in Basel and Brussels should provide more ammunition for them to employ.

As noted above, there is no guarantee that systemic or individual bank problems can be detected, much less addressed. Not only did the total collapse of systemic liquidity surprise even the experts in 2007, but the subsequent failure and nationalisation of Northern Rock also undermined the maxim that retail deposits are sticky.

The system can do better!

A final word on the subject of effectiveness comes from Charles Littrell of APRA:

> "Our experience suggests that having competent people, good systems, etc are all important, but the relevant peer regulators have these tools. A culture of constant, mild, but effective intervention differentiates successful prudential regulation from cultures which have to convince themselves to intervene, often at the enforcement stage."

Redefining 'regulation' and 'supervision'

WE STARTED OUR RESEARCH with a simple definition of regulation (the formulation of rules) and supervision (the enforcing of the rules). Most of our sources agreed with this basic distinction, but added a few very useful caveats.

First, there is a strong argument that fewer, simple rules or principles that 'Granny can understand' are better than a rulebook of hundreds of pages. Several interviewees commented that a multiplicity of rules, as opposed to basic principles, simply attracts the inevitable avoidance tactics. As for the distinction between 'principles-based' and 'rules-based', they are both useful, but the key is the ability to enforce them effectively.

Second, what has been missing in so many regulatory structures is the brainpower that stands between rule formulation and actual supervision – what one of our interviewees calls 'the brains in the middle'. This is the function that conceives and carries out systemic research, stress testing and actual dialogue with the bankers. It can be included in either 'regulation' or 'supervision', but it has been the missing link in so many banking failures. Again, there is no guarantee that this unit – or anyone – will identify the next crisis, but at least the function is acknowledged and is in place.

Third, for many regulators the supervision function itself, whether embedded in the banks or outside, has morphed into a compliance or audit function, often totally divorced from the core mission of risk assessment and enforcement. Not only may this not make best use of the skills available, but it appears ill-equipped to identify systemic or other problems requiring top management attention.

Finally, the experience of successful regulators is that close contact and sharing of insights is needed between the top management of a bank and its regulator. Such a matching of talents and perspectives seems to be necessary both in identifying problems as well as enforcing a regulatory decision. Thus the UK FSA has been criticised for the lack of such high level dialogue, whereas in the three case studies of Australia, Canada and Norway the central dialogue was between bank CEOs and the top regulators.

Loughborough University's David Llewellyn sums up how best regulatory practice has evolved as a result of the crisis:

> "Under Fed Chairman Greenspan, the view was that, regarding asset price bubbles, you're better off dealing with

a problem after it has occurred rather than trying to spot it. All that has changed, along with the theory of 'rational expectations' and 'efficient markets'. The intellectual climate that dominated the 1990s and early part of the 21st century has changed.

"Supervision is now more broadly defined than simply 'are the rules being followed?' It's also taking an overall view of the bank and potential risks. Pillar 2 in Basel II was hijacked by Pillar 1 – the focus on Tier 1 capital. The crisis was not a problem of regulation, nor are structural reforms like a new Glass-Steagall the answer. If you can't have an ideal world of perfect regulation, it might be better to adopt a fundamentally different approach: fairly simple rules bolstered with emphasis on Pillar 2. The real issue is the mindset of the supervisor!"

The need for quality in regulatory and supervisory skills

WE BEGAN THIS RESEARCH with the view that regulatory agencies were largely staffed by bureaucrats and bean-counters – fortunately a total mistake! These people certainly exist, but the problem lies elsewhere. As so many of our sources pointed out, the problem starts at the top, with their mandate of risk analysis and remedies.

If there is any durable lesson from the recent crisis, it is that the core mission of the agency is to identify and manage risk in the banking system, not to enforce rules about accounting or administrative practices.

If this mandate is clear, the actual staffing issues fall into place. We were impressed by comments in our interviews about the availability of the necessary brainpower, career commitment and other qualities, in particular in the central banking community, which seems to attract some of the best and brightest in government service. When coupled with the availability of experienced and committed banking talent in markets like Norway, recent efforts to improve compensation scales and other measures undertaken, we are less concerned about the 'people' issue.

Politics – the core issue

THE CORE PROBLEM remains politics – the enemy of bank regulation!

There is no simple solution in a democratic society to the problem faced by regulators in markets like the US, Spain and Germany where voters, and therefore legislators, can be influenced by banks and bank owners.

It is particularly painful in the US, the world's largest and most sophisticated banking system. The only remedy that presents itself is to increase the credibility of the agency and its management – just as so many central banks have done in the macro-economic world of money supply and interest rates. But it has taken decades in the US for voters to acknowledge, at least in principle, that such decisions should be taken by the Federal Reserve system – and still Chairman Ben Bernanke has difficulty in being reappointed to his post!

Yet both types of institutions – not only the successful regulators quoted above, but also senior individual bank regulators – have succeeded in winning credibility among voters. Mario Draghi and Jean Claude Trichet are highly regarded central bankers as well as skilled politicians in their own right.

How can this aura of competence be extended to bank regulators? It already has. As mentioned in Chapter 7, the *Financial Times* in January 2010 already published a laudatory article on OSFI's Julie Dickson. One solution is obvious: merge the separate bank regulator into the highly respected central bank. Quite apart from the views of politicians in markets like the UK and Germany who have recommended this solution, there is the rationale that a career path in such a respected institution could well ensure a higher level of skills committed to regulation. This also coincides with the view that macro-economic responsibilities for interest rates and money supply can fit comfortably with parallel macro-prudential responsibilities for bank regulation.

Amidst all the criticism of politicians meddling with bank regulation, one positive exception is cited by Jean-Louis Fort, former Commission Bancaire executive in Paris. Referring to President Sarkozy's declaration at the height of the banking crisis that "no depositor in a French bank will lose a single Euro", Fort observes that:

> "In normal times, political intervention is not a good idea, but in a crisis it can be critical. It had to be done, despite the lack of a legal basis, as depositors were preparing to withdraw their money. It was intelligent and necessary at a time when regulators can't do it."

And finally, there is the point made by so many of the successful specialist bank regulators that a critical success factor in their work is effective collaboration and information-sharing with their peers in the central bank. Whatever the merits of any organisational structure, it is likely that the new model bank regulation will involve much closer collaboration between central banks and bank regulators, if not an actual merger between the two.

A level playing field for bank regulators?

WILL THERE BE A SMOOTH INTERFACE – or 'level playing field' – between bank regulators around the world?

Our conversations with national regulators engaged in deep debate in Basel and Brussels in search of this uniform approach to regulation all confirm the challenge they face in aligning both rules and execution across national boundaries. In the EU, for example, there is little indication that the 49 EU national regulators in the financial sector will change their ways of working. One such regulator interviewed for this book, when asked what would change for him in the future, replied: "Nothing – just more work!"

The evidence points to continued differences in approach, quality and external constraints. The debate in early 2010 over bonuses and taxes on banks accepting government funds is an indication of the problems in imposing a single global approach. But the overall performance of bank regulation should improve even without this uniformity.

Individual regulators will continue to vary in effectiveness, political forces will still intervene, and gaps between regulators will still exist. But organisations such as the FSB and CEBS should help change the regulatory game for the better.

The danger of over-regulation

What former FSA regulator Clive Briault calls the "more of everything" approach to bank regulation is a real threat to its future effectiveness. In the current scramble for solutions, several of our sources expressed the concern that many such measures, often with little relation to the risk management problems associated with the recent crisis, will find their way to the statute books.

Such a wave of new initiatives will make the execution task even more difficult for overworked supervisors. Thus, the anger at bank bonuses may result in detailed review of such compensation schemes at such agencies as the UK FSA, which already suffers from regulatory overload.

An indication of the universal concern for over-regulation is the 2009 survey carried out globally with a wide spectrum of bankers, regulators, consultants and others by the Centre for the Study of Financial Innovation (CSFI), a London think-tank which publishes an annual report on the concerns of these various constituencies. Not surprisingly, at the top of the bankers' latest worry list are two topics: political interference and too much regulation. Perhaps more interesting is the 'observers' category – analysts and consultants – which also placed political interference at the top of their concerns. And for the regulators themselves, political interference came second only to credit risk!

And also lost in the shuffle may be the need to steer that delicate path between innovation and rules. As the sub-prime and other 'innovative' products showed during the crisis, a product which serves a useful purpose can easily be transformed into a toxic one. Thus securitisation is widely agreed to be a good thing in principle, yet carried to extremes of leverage and asset quality, it can be dangerous. And identifying the toxic from the useful is not a simple task, in particular in a bull market.

The so-called 'law of unintended consequences' is widely and justifiably invoked as regulators struggle to devise the perfect regulatory framework. *The Economist*'s Buttonwood column (*The Economist*, January 30, 2010) summarises eloquently the dangers:

"All these examples illustrate the general rule that capital, like water, tends to flow around obstacles. Try to dam its movement at one point, and slowly but remorselessly it will find its way around. ... The unregulated part of the finance sector will become more important systemically, something the authorities may regret when the next crisis comes along."

The role of bank management

Finally, bank management, not regulation, is still the first line of defence.

Blaming the regulators for bank failures is still an issue. Witnessing the grilling of Washington regulators on nationwide television in recent months is not an inspiring event. Politicians and voters still shoot the wrong messenger, rather than the management team which drove a bank into the government's arms. So many of our interviewees pointed out that the purpose of effective regulation is not to replace management, but to take timely steps to limit losses.

Appendix: Extracts from Pillar 2 of the Basel II Accord

Searching finance

Part 3: The Second Pillar – Supervisory Review Process

719. This section discusses the key principles of supervisory review, risk management guidance and supervisory transparency and accountability produced by the Committee with respect to banking risks, including guidance relating to, among other things, the treatment of interest rate risk in the banking book, credit risk (stress testing, definition of default, residual risk, and credit concentration risk), operational risk, enhanced cross-border communication and cooperation, and securitisation.

I. Importance of supervisory review

720. The supervisory review process of the Framework is intended not only to ensure that banks have adequate capital to support all the risks in their business, but also to encourage banks to develop and use better risk management techniques in monitoring and managing their risks.

721. The supervisory review process recognises the responsibility of bank management in developing an internal capital assessment process and setting capital targets that are commensurate with the bank's risk profile and control environment. In the Framework, bank management continues to bear responsibility for ensuring that the bank has adequate capital to support its risks beyond the core minimum requirements.

722. Supervisors are expected to evaluate how well banks are assessing their capital needs relative to their risks and to intervene, where appropriate. This interaction is intended to foster an active dialogue between banks and supervisors such that when deficiencies are identified, prompt and decisive action can be taken to reduce risk or restore capital. Accordingly, supervisors

may wish to adopt an approach to focus more intensely on those banks with risk profiles or operational experience that warrants such attention.

723. The Committee recognises the relationship that exists between the amount of capital held by the bank against its risks and the strength and effectiveness of the bank's risk management and internal control processes. However, increased capital should not be viewed as the only option for addressing increased risks confronting the bank. Other means for addressing risk, such as strengthening risk management, applying internal limits, strengthening the level of provisions and reserves, and improving internal controls, must also be considered. Furthermore, capital should not be regarded as a substitute for addressing fundamentally inadequate control or risk management processes.

724. There are three main areas that might be particularly suited to treatment under Pillar 2: risks considered under Pillar 1 that are not fully captured by the Pillar 1 process (e.g. credit concentration risk); those factors not taken into account by the Pillar 1 process (e.g. interest rate risk in the banking book, business and strategic risk); and factors external to the bank (e.g. business cycle effects). A further important aspect of Pillar 2 is the assessment of compliance with the minimum standards and disclosure requirements of the more advanced methods in Pillar 1, in particular the IRB framework for credit risk and the Advanced Measurement Approaches for operational risk. Supervisors must ensure that these requirements are being met, both as qualifying criteria and on a continuing basis.

II. Four key principles of supervisory review

725. The Committee has identified four key principles of supervisory review, which complement those outlined in the

extensive supervisory guidance that has been developed by the Committee, the keystone of which is the Core Principles for Effective Banking Supervision and the Core Principles Methodology.110 A list of the specific guidance relating to the management of banking risks is provided at the end of this Part of the Framework.

Principle 1: Banks should have a process for assessing their overall capital adequacy in relation to their risk profile and a strategy for maintaining their capital levels.

726. Banks must be able to demonstrate that chosen internal capital targets are well founded and that these targets are consistent with their overall risk profile and current operating environment. In assessing capital adequacy, bank management needs to be mindful of the particular stage of the business cycle in which the bank is operating. Rigorous, forward-looking stress testing that identifies possible events or changes in market conditions that could adversely impact the bank should be performed. Bank management clearly bears primary responsibility for ensuring that the bank has adequate capital to support its risks.

727. The five main features of a rigorous process are as follows:

Board and senior management oversight;

Sound capital assessment;

Comprehensive assessment of risks;

Monitoring and reporting; and

Internal control review.

Principle 2: Supervisors should review and evaluate banks' internal capital adequacy assessments and strategies, as well as their ability to monitor and ensure their compliance with regulatory capital ratios. Supervisors should take appropriate supervisory action if they are not satisfied with the result of this process.

746. The supervisory authorities should regularly review the process by which a bank assesses its capital adequacy, risk position, resulting capital levels, and quality of capital held. Supervisors should also evaluate the degree to which a bank has in place a sound internal process to assess capital adequacy. The emphasis of the review should be on the quality of the bank's risk management and controls and should not result in supervisors functioning as bank management. The periodic review can involve some combination of:

On-site examinations or inspections;

Off-site review;

Discussions with bank management;

Review of work done by external auditors (provided it is adequately focused on the necessary capital issues); and

Periodic reporting.

Principle 3: Supervisors should expect banks to operate above the minimum regulatory capital ratios and should have the ability to require banks to hold capital in excess of the minimum.

757. Pillar 1 capital requirements will include a buffer for uncertainties surrounding the Pillar 1 regime that affect the banking population as a whole. Bank-specific uncertainties will be treated under Pillar 2. It is anticipated that such buffers under Pillar 1 will be set to provide reasonable assurance that a bank with good internal systems and controls, a well-diversified risk profile and a business profile well covered by the Pillar 1 regime, and which operates with capital equal to Pillar 1 requirements, will meet the minimum goals for soundness embodied in Pillar 1. However, supervisors will need to consider whether the particular features of the markets for which they are responsible are adequately covered. Supervisors will typically require (or en-

courage) banks to operate with a buffer, over and above the Pillar 1 standard. Banks should maintain this buffer for a combination of the following:

(a) Pillar 1 minimums are anticipated to be set to achieve a level of bank creditworthiness in markets that is below the level of creditworthiness sought by many banks for their own reasons. For example, most international banks appear to prefer to be highly rated by internationally recognised rating agencies. Thus, banks are likely to choose to operate above Pillar 1 minimums for competitive reasons.

(b) In the normal course of business, the type and volume of activities will change, as will the different risk exposures, causing fluctuations in the overall capital ratio.

(c) It may be costly for banks to raise additional capital, especially if this needs to be done quickly or at a time when market conditions are unfavourable.

(d) For banks to fall below minimum regulatory capital requirements is a serious matter. It may place banks in breach of the relevant law and/or prompt non-discretionary corrective action on the part of supervisors.

(e) There may be risks, either specific to individual banks, or more generally to an economy at large, that are not taken into account in Pillar 1.

Principle 4: Supervisors should seek to intervene at an early stage to prevent capital from falling below the minimum levels required to support the risk characteristics of a particular bank and should require rapid remedial action if capital is not maintained or restored.

759. Supervisors should consider a range of options if they become concerned that a bank is not meeting the requirements embodied in the supervisory principles outlined above. These actions may include intensifying the monitoring of the bank, restricting the payment of dividends, requiring the bank to pre-

pare and implement a satisfactory capital adequacy restoration plan, and requiring the bank to raise additional capital immediately. Supervisors should have the discretion to use the tools best suited to the circumstances of the bank and its operating environment.

760. The permanent solution to banks' difficulties is not always increased capital. However, some of the required measures (such as improving systems and controls) may take a period of time to implement. Therefore, increased capital might be used as an interim measure while permanent measures to improve the bank's position are being put in place. Once these permanent measures have been put in place and have been seen by supervisors to be effective, the interim increase in capital requirements can be removed.

Bibliography

THIS BIBLIOGRAPHY INCLUDES A FRACTION, albeit in our view a significant one, of the published material in the public domain which is relevant to our objective. It includes what we regard as required reading for anyone seeking to place the recent crisis in a historical context, such as Charles Kindleberger's classic 'Manias, Panics and Crashes', Robert Shiller's 'Irrational Exuberance', and JK Galbraith's 'The Great Crash of 1929'.

Another must-read story of the tumult itself is Andrew Sorkin's remarkable account of the crisis in Washington, 'Too Big to Fail', while an excellent analysis by a former senior FSA regulator is Clive Briault's 'Fixing Regulation'.

The balance of the bibliography consists of a sampling of historical data on bank regulation such as research from Professor James Barth (a key US government advisor and Lowder Eminent Scholar in Finance at Auburn University and a Senior Fellow at the Milken Institute) with special emphasis on regulatory issues), and recent policy statements by such leading regulators as the Basel Committee, the European Union, and the US Federal Reserve. Along with similar statements from earlier Basel II documents, this is intended to give the reader a sampling of the suggested approach summarised in the phrase 'macro-prudential regulation'.

Barth, James R, Caprio Gerald, and Levine, Ross: *Rethinking Bank Regulation: Till Angels Govern*

Bernanke, Ben: *Testimony before the US Senate Committee on Banking*, December 2009

Borio, Claudio: Implementing the Macro-prudential Approach to Financial Regulation and supervision, Banque de France *Financial Stability Review*, September 2009

Briault, Clive: *Fixing Regulation*, CSFI (Centre for the Study of Financial Innovation, London, October, 2009

Credit Sights: *The Decade's Top 10 Credit Events*, London, January 2010

Draghi, Mario: *Challenges to Financial Stability and the Proposals of the Financial Stability Board*; presented in November 2009 to the Conference of ECB-CFS Research Network

Freeland, Chrystia: What can Canada Teach the World, Financial Times, January 2010

Gerding, Erik: *Lombard Street – Special Meltdown Issue*, London, September 2009

Kindleberger, Charles P, *Manias, Panics and Crashes: A History of Financial Crises*, Wiley Investment Classics, 2000

Shiller, Robert: *Irrational Exuberance*

www.ingramcontent.com/pod-product-compliance
Ingram Content Group UK Ltd.
Pitfield, Milton Keynes, MK11 3LW, UK
UKHW040227290926
15471UKWH00001B/32

9 781907 72000